Praise for Storying Silence

"Jane's passionate and courageous call to voice is for every woman who has her story to tell (and that would be all of us). She is a powerful, compassionate, and skilled guide in Storying Silence to lead us from patriarchal silencing to flowering with the hard won meaningfulness of our own lives and stories. Through the juicy creative exercises that call forth your authentic voice, be ready to take ownership of your own life narrative, and join the growing tribe of women who refuse to be silenced any more."

— Melissa Gayle West, author of *Exploring the Labyrinth: A Guide for Healing and Spiritual Growth, Silver Linings: The Power of Trauma to Transform Your Life,* and *Soulful Living: The Process of Transformation*

"*Storying Silence* is far more than a workbook; it's a profound (Wo)Manifesto dedicated to the vital journey of Un-Silencing the Self. Arriving at a crucial moment, it serves as both a wise guide and a practical toolkit for remembering what has been dis-remembered in women's lives—on both an individual and collective level. This work stands as a source of bold, creative enCOURAGEment for those ready to embrace the struggle (and triumph) of healing over silent conformity. I wholeheartedly recommend it for group exploration—whether in therapy, women's circles, or book and writing clubs. The act of sharing and witnessing our voices, stories, and truths holds transformative power: it deepens our connection to ourselves and to each other, celebrating our courage and beauty. By uncovering the mechanisms that enforce silence and submission, this resource empowers us to become active wayfarers—not just for ourselves, but for our daughters, our communities, and future generations—realizing the dreams of those who came before us."

— Linda Abrams, LCSW-R, or Licensed Clinical Social Worker

"*Storying Silence* invites women to reclaim their voices, power and sovereignty through the transformative act of writing. This compassionate guide provides a path to creating personal sanctuaries where women can safely confront, celebrate and share their sacred truths, break free from silence and rediscover their own inherent strengths. Clark calls upon women of all colors and ethnicities to write together, to create together, to deal with all those experiences that might otherwise go unstoried. *Storying Silence* is a call to honor the journey and empower oneself to write authentically and boldly."

— Galen Leonhardy, Professor of English, Black Hawk College. Author of *Skipping Stones,* and "The Small Pond: A Play on Racism and Antiracist Teaching"

In this workbook, Clark takes a developmental approach in presenting a variety of topics a woman experiences in her life to help her see how she has been "silenced" by cultural forces. By providing historical and modern contextual stories, along with provocative writing prompts, the reader is encouraged to begin her "unsilencing," to own and write her authentic stories based on her lived experiences.

—Mary Aebischer, PhD, educator, and scholar in women's movements and consciousness raising groups

STORYING SILENCE

A Writing Workbook to Restore
Your Voice & Reclaim
Your Sovereignty

JANE CLARK

Writing Brave LLC
1940 Palmer Avenue, #1032
Larchmont NY 10538

www.writingbravepress.com

Distributed by IngramSpark

Cover and Text Design: Melissa Williams Design

Copyeditor: Meghan Muldowney

Author Photos: Samantha Wilson

Library of Congress Cataloging-in-Publication Data available.

ISBN 979-8-9918111-3-2 (Paperback)
ISBN 979-8-9918111-4-9 (Ebook)

First Edition

I dedicate this book to the Wade Women of West Texas,
who carried untold stories for centuries.

Contents

Section 4: *Recognition—Honoring Your Hard Work*

A Note Before You Begin

Dear Reader,

As I write this note to you, I'm watching the world descend into chaos following the installation of a president who, as a sexual predator, is a threat to all our safety and a Supreme Court ruling that has taken away women's rights to bodily autonomy. While watching powerful institutions rip away rights we've had for 50 years, I worry that women may miss seeing the harm inflicted by news reports that emphasize the force used against us, while portraying us as voiceless victims. It's imperative that we recognize this as a move that further erodes our rights by interpreting our experiences through the lens of a dominant white male narrative which renders us powerless, unable to resist oppression. A myth that tells us we are safer when we align with old ideas promulgated by the patriarchy.

This is *our* story to tell. Any effort to tell it on our behalf threatens to dispossess us, disappear us, and silence us. Giving up narrative control to the people who are depriving us of our freedoms allows them to bury us beneath the lines of dominant tales that reinforce the power of the elite. But we must do more than defy this form of oppression; we need to see the systemic set of rules, beliefs, thoughts, behaviors, policies, and laws that have not only silenced us but have encouraged us to silence one another.

Silence is experienced unevenly, impacting women in different ways, depending on gender, race, class, and social status. As white women, we must confront the fact that we've been co-opted by an authoritarian system that rewards us for failing to acknowledge the stories of oppression told by our sisters of color. It's a system which will make it impossible for us to work together to reach greater equality. If we are going to unsilence ourselves and restore our autonomy, we must refuse to believe the myth that we need the protection of a patriarchal system that keeps us separated from one another. As activist Lilla Watson observed, we can only reclaim our autonomy if we acknowledge that our freedom is bound up in the liberty of all.

This workbook is a **call-to-arms** to all women to gather in circles to create a collection of tales that represents our experiences in the world. It is a call to create an oeuvre of works that subverts the tales being told about us and replaces them with stories we write in our words. It's a call to strike out and break old rules that have kept us separated and silent for too long. By writing our stories in our own words we can resist attempts to erase us and begin to establish our place in history, one tale at a time.

The material in this workbook is based on thirty years of research, teaching, and leading writing workshops with women. It is intended for all women from every culture and race, as well as anyone who identifies with a group that has been excluded from the dominant conversation. I hope you find it to be a useful guide as you work your way back into voice, through the process of writing your story. My desire is that my words will inspire you to undertake a **journey of liberation**.

> *"Moving from silence into speech is. . . . a gesture of defiance that heals, that makes new life and new growth possible. It is that act of speech, of "talking back," that is no mere gesture of empty words, that is the expression of our movement from object to subject—the liberated voice."*

—bell hooks, Talking Back, Thinking Feminist, Thinking Black, 1989

Come sit with me for a while and turn your silence into a story. There's space here for silence, for grief, for laughter, and for the unsaid to appear in the slowly returning sound of your voice. Sovereign, steady, yours.

Sincerely, *Jane*

Rage

I am
Pretty
Damned
Exhausted
By well-meaning men
Family
Lovers
Friends

Making excuses
Explanations
Exceptions
For the reasons that
"I'm not like them."

And trying to
Enumerate
The reasons why
Or how
A woman does
What she does
Or says
What she says

Like they have a clue
How she feels
What motivates
Or discourages
Or what even
She is capable of

How
Fucking
Dare
They
Put me in this box?

And then pretend
They don't how
Why I rage
In their cage.

Jeannine Burkholder
January 26, 2025

Section 1:
Introduction

The (Wo)Man in the Mirror: *Struggling with My Own Silence*

Your Invitation: *Engaging in the Movement*

Your Call: *Seeing Harsh Truths*

The (Wo)Man in the Mirror: Struggling with My Own Silence

More than fifteen years ago, my former husband died in a sudden, violent way, and the shock of his death pushed me into such a place of darkness. It seemed to take away my own life, leaving me unable to teach, write, or even to speak. When the Chair of the English Department at the university suggested a leave of absence from my teaching job, I jumped at the opportunity. But a couple of weeks later, I slid into an ocean of grief so deep, I could barely keep my head above water. At the end of each afternoon, as I sat by my large dining room window, watching the sky take back the day, I felt myself fading with the light as it dropped below the horizon, and I wondered if I'd ever be able to return to the classroom or do research again. One morning, about two months into my leave, I stood in my kitchen, drinking reheated coffee, shuffling through unopened mail when I found an envelope with a return address of "Narrative Research Conference," which caught my attention. I grabbed my reading glasses, opened the letter, unfolded it, and read the first line aloud.

"Congratulations. We're writing to invite you to speak at the Interdisciplinary Conference on Narrative Research." The event, at St. Thomas University in New Brunswick, Canada, would be centered on the power of story to shape our lives. As I read the details, it hit me just how much I missed my old life. For years, stories had been at the center of my career, the themes in the classes I taught, and the subjects of my graduate work. In all honesty, they helped me to make sense of the way my life seemed to unfold in one dramatic episode after another. I told myself that speaking at this conference would pull me out of my funk. Just thinking about it sparked my excitement, and I sat down that evening at my desk to work on my talk.

I came up with the title, "(WO)man in the Mirror," based on the Michael Jackson song, "Man in the Mirror," with the idea of showing how narrative researchers can become so enchanted by stories that we wander deep into the center and lose sight of ourselves. I fantasized that speaking to a group of theorists–who also studied story–would be my entry back into an active professional life and a way out of my grief-stricken silence. As I wrote, a desire stirred in me to step back into the creative state that had defined most of my life, to reclaim what my mother had called my "crazy-wild imagination." That's when the big idea hit me. Instead of flying to Canada, I'd turn the trip into an adventure by driving from my home in Pennsylvania up the northeastern coast to the university.

The day before the conference began, I packed my bag, jumped into the car, and drove for 10 hours without stopping through New York, Massachusetts, New Hampshire, and Maine. I was excited to be putting miles between me and my tragic loss, leaving behind the sorrow that had become my uninvited escort in the past few months. I reached the Canadian border at about 1 a.m. and presented the guard with my passport and driver's license. He asked about the reason for my visit.

"I'm presenting at an academic conference," I told him.

The look on his face told me he didn't approve, so I wasn't surprised when he told me to turn back.

"This is not a safe highway to travel in the middle of the night," the guard said.

"I have to go on," I protested. "I have to be in Fredericton–115 miles away–in just a few hours." He explained that the trip would take me deep into the wilderness of the Wabanaki-Acadian Forest, where long stretches of highway were separated by only one or two rest stops.

"Nothing will be open at this time of night," he said. I shrugged. Then, to make sure I understood, he added, "It will be very dark, so you'll have to watch for bear and moose on the road."

The guard tried again, warning me. "This is a desolate area where several indigenous women have disappeared in recent months. The body of one young woman was discovered near here just a few weeks ago."

I should have been intimidated but his caution made me more determined to continue. *After all,* I thought, *this is my journey out of the story grief had been telling about me, a gesture at reclaiming my life.* For months, I'd been roaming across a landscape of sadness, and I was intrigued by the idea of entering into a different time zone and crossing geographic and cultural boundaries. Driving into the darkness, moving through an ancient forest, and emerging on the other side felt like a ritualized way to come out of the cave I'd been living in. I jumped back into the car and drove away with my phone charged and my car loaded with sugary snacks to keep me awake. Running across a moose or any animal on an isolated highway didn't seem very frightening.

A few miles down the highway, I drove beneath a canopy of evergreen trees, their heavy branches hanging over the road, making shadows dance in front of the car. I opened my sunroof and watched for openings between the boughs, which seemed to cut the moon into slivers that bled across the sky. Stars peppered the ceiling above and silence encased the car as I drove deeper into the land named for the Wabanaki tribe. I looked out the front window but saw no movement except layers of foggy vapor suspended in the air, broken up by my car as it pushed forward. When a glint of moonlight struck the windshield, I shivered, remembering the guard's report of missing women. I wondered if I'd passed the area in the woods where the body of the youngest victim had been found. Leaning forward, I looked into the mist, then, checked the rear-view and side-view mirrors. Nothing was there. Another flash of light took me back four months, to the night I'd driven home from the university, following the moon as it lit up back roads, and arrived home, to find my husband dead.

"I'm safe," I told myself, pressing the gas pedal down as much as I dared.

It was still dark when I arrived in Fredericton about three hours later, so I checked into a Holiday Inn, took a short nap, showered, got dressed, and drove to the university a few blocks from the

St. John River. My body felt like it was still floating through the dark world of the forest, but the morning sunlight hitting tall buildings in the city brought me back. I drove through the gate fronting the campus and found a parking space in the shade of a red maple tree near the front of the brick Neo-Georgian style conference center, where my group was scheduled to speak.

Before leaving home, I'd read about the university, which was named for St. Thomas Aquinas and built on land taken from indigenous tribes by the French and English. When procured by the Basilian Order of the Catholic Church, it was to become the site of a school to train diocesan priests. In the same area, the Church built a dozen or so Indian day schools, where indigenous children were separated from their families, then trained and taken to local farms to work as indentured servants. As I opened the huge glass doors and stepped over the threshold, the weight of this history struck me, and I was aware that, as a widow struggling to find her footing, I was not unlike a foreigner who had lost her place in the world.

Within a few minutes, people began to arrive in the large open conference room. Technicians set up equipment, testing microphones, placing computers on long tables, and opening up a large screen in the front of the room.

A woman wearing a name badge attached to a lanyard came up to me. "Are you here to watch the presenters?" she asked.

"I *am* a presenter," I retorted.

"Oh." She looked surprised, then showed me the list where I pointed to my name.

"Here's your packet of information. I'm the chair's secretary and I can help you get settled in."

I thanked her and walked to the back of the room to the catering table where I got a cup of coffee and a cheese-filled Danish roll. The air in the room felt heavy, full of somber energy. Not wanting to lose the edge of my excitement, I told myself the apprehension I felt came from being tired, after driving through the night with very little sleep and no food. As more people arrived, a soft din of conversation began to build. No one was loud; after all, they were academics. In fact, the voices seemed low and dull, and I leaned in, trying to connect with the energy.

Joining a small group in the corner, I introduced myself.

"Do you still teach?" asked a young man. My throat tightened.

"Yes, and I also hold an administrative position at the university."

"Oh, that's just great," he added, too enthusiastically.

I knew he was already spinning a story in his head about me, the woman he met at a conference–*near his mother's age*–who was still actively working. Within a few minutes, the program started, and we took our seats to watch as one academic after another droned on about abstract theories, while moderators kept notes and audience members asked questions.

Two hours later, my legs started to ache from the long drive. I yawned. The voices of speakers began to fade in and out of my awareness. My eyes felt heavy. I caught myself and straightened my spine. *This is my comeback*, I thought, as I sat up taller in the chair. One of the young

5

professors must have seen my head falling forward a bit. He reached over and patted me on the shoulder. I wanted to growl at him but decided to hold on to the energy for my presentation.

Two men, whose names appeared on the program ahead of mine, rose to speak. They introduced themselves and explained their backgrounds: one from philosophy, the other from English literature. It's true that academics study the most obscure topics, but even I was shocked when the title of their study flashed across the oversized screen: "The Disorganized Stories Told by Sex Workers in Bolivia."

My body stiffened. I was sure all the oxygen was sucked out of the room but when I looked around, no one seemed to react. They took turns speaking, the monotone voice of the youngest professor clashing against the discordant tone of his colleague. I watched the red bow tie bounce up and down on the Adam's apple of the youngest as he spoke about the women in the study. *My God,* I wondered, *where is the decency here? Why is this an acceptable topic?* Two charmed, privileged white men sharing stories they had–in my opinion–stolen from women. The taste of burned coffee rose in my mouth and I swallowed. More upsetting than the topic itself was the way they spoke about the participants, as though they were laboratory animals held captive, their behavior codified, their stories classified like notes written by a botanist studying organisms in a clinical setting. Anger began to build, and I covered my mouth with my hand to keep myself from speaking.

I thought back to the warnings of the border guard who, just a few hours earlier, told me to watch for wildlife on the dark road, recalling his description of "unfortunate indigenous women" who "disappeared" in this area. Even the word "disappeared" triggered me. *They had been abducted,* I thought. Women, who were among thousands whose cases remain unsolved as of this writing. Reports of their vanishing were likely also buried on the pages of an official report in the hands of an investigator with the Royal Canadian Mounted Police. Unread.

The two professors stopped speaking. It was my turn. I took a deep breath, and I walked to the front of the room, more aware of being a single, mature-aged woman than I should have been. Aware of my small stature. My hair, my clothing. Whether or not I appeared to be tired. I knew I'd have to shift the tone in the room and take back control of the narrative.

Can I do this? I wondered. *Reset the tone in the proverbial ivory tower, a space where the stories of white men ruled?* The room felt stiff, unyielding. Not even the walls seemed to be willing to listen to me.

I took a deep breath, gritted my teeth, and set my jaw. I placed my report on the podium, adjusted the height, looked down at the first page, raised the mic, and took another deep breath.

"Good morning…" As I began to speak, my voice cracked. I opened the bottle of water I had carried up with me, took a sip, and began again. "Good morning…"

I felt disoriented. *Focus,* I reminded myself. But focusing took me straight to the feeling I'd been trying to swallow all morning. Anger. In fact, it roused an intense rage. I wanted to explode, to yell, "This is how women lose our voices. We become the subjects of academic reports written about us. We're turned into secondary characters in the history of patriarchal institutions that enslave and farm out our children. Our lives are reduced to stories of caution used by law enforcement to frighten other women, stories about women trying to survive in war-torn countries. Stories told in ways that obscure us."

Instead of screaming, I forced myself to look up at the audience and smile. I knew it wouldn't work. When I opened my mouth to speak…the tears started. *Oh, no, I thought. I can't cry.* Desperate to continue, I tried once again to speak but this time, I blurted out, "My husband died a few months ago." *Damn it. I hadn't wanted to say that.*

Tears, again. They were hot, stinging drops filled with what felt like tiny pieces of salt cutting through the film coating my eyeballs. My eyes felt like they were on fire. Then, the oddest thing happened. My vision cleared a bit and when I looked up, I saw myself as "The (Wo)Man in the Mirror." The one who came to talk about the problem of losing objectivity in research, but who could no longer keep quiet about the injustice, the unfairness, and the immorality of stealing women's stories and silencing us. Now, I didn't care if I made my original point. I didn't care if I'd cried. Nor if I'd blown my re-entry into academia.

I wanted out. Out of the building, out of the conference. Out of Canada. Out of my career in a patriarchal institution where women's stories were not valued.

I continued on, giving just the highlights of my research on the way women encounter silence, including the sources I'd used in my paper. But I didn't want to share any more of my work with this group, so I told them, "In the interest of time, I'll stop here." I said that I'd provide a copy of my talk to anyone who wanted to know more about my research. I thanked them, turned off the microphone, and gathered up my things. As I started moving toward the door, two female presenters who had spoken earlier cut me off.

"You're so courageous," said one, as she reached out to hug me.

"It's very brave of you to try to present so soon after your husband's death," offered the other one.

I didn't want to be consoled. I didn't want to be talked down off the ledge of fury where I'd climbed. I'd come too far to let anyone else characterize my experience. So, I smiled and walked away, as fast as I could, past people gathering their belongings, past the technicians taking down equipment, past the refreshment table and caterers.

In the back of my mind, the words echoed, "Watch out for moose on the road." I thought, *In my mind, the real danger to me is not in the forest. It isn't in the wilderness with ghosts and animals. It's in this hall where women's stories are buried.*

When I got to the car, I sat in the quiet and began to breathe deeply. After a couple of minutes, I felt the urge to move. I started the engine and drove out of the parking lot, away from the campus, out of the city of Fredericton, in the direction of the forest, where I'd finally be free to open my mouth and yell. I fantasized about the sound of my voice rising up into the sky and blending with the wind to create a new sound. A battle cry.

Two and a half hours later when I arrived at the Wabanaki Forest, I was surprised at how different it looked and felt during the day. Not as placid as the previous night when I seemed to glide through the trees, enfolded in the dark as though held in the earth's womb. The sun poked in and out of clouds; the sharp wind blew the leaves off maple trees and threatened to bend the trunks of the balsams. The world felt hard, cold. *Where was the mystical forest that had drawn me into its center to listen to its magical stories?*

Thinking I'd find a spot on the highway that looked inviting, I picked up speed and didn't stop until I reached the state of Maine, where I exited the highway to find the overlook at Baxter State Park. I searched for Mt. Katahdin, the northernmost peak on the Appalachian Trail and the highest point in the state. When it came into view, I found a place to park my car, got out, and walked over to get a closer look. Standing in the shadow of the peak, I began to feel again the gravity of the stories of women whose lives had been erased. Then more rage. Powerful enough to cause an avalanche, pushing heavy rocks and chunks of ice down the side of a mountain.

In the distance, I thought I heard a sound like muffled thunder, so I quickly walked back down the trail, unlocked the car door, and got inside. I drove toward the highway and, as I pulled away, I caught a glimpse of something moving just off the side of the road. I turned around just in time to see a bull moose with an antler rack that seemed to span more than six feet. He was huge. Majestic, standing at the edge of the forest. But it was more than his size that caught my attention. From within the silence of my car, I saw his nostrils flare and heard his deep, bassy roar. A sound I will never forget.

Your Invitation: Joining the Movement

You do not have to be an accomplished writer to use this workbook; you merely have to have a story to tell and a desire to tell it. I have put together this material with the belief that we are all story carriers, who have untold tales waiting for an invitation to guide us through the transformative process of making meaning out of our life experiences. Stories that want to help us respond to the forces that threaten to silence us by monitoring our speech and punishing us when we defy oppression by standing up and speaking out.

The exercises on the following pages are meant to help you step into your stories and let them guide you back into ownership of your narrative. When you begin to write in response to the prompts, you'll be joining a tribe of women raising our pens like swords against the campaign to undermine our autonomy. You'll be using writing to cast an incantation, to articulate your expectation to be remembered as a woman who spoke up during a time in history when it was not always safe to do so. You'll be merging with other writers who are insisting on using our own interpretations of our life experiences to create chronicles of our presence during this period. You'll be storying yourself out of silence.

Silencing women is an ancient practice. The pages of western literature are stained with the blood of women who have been silenced using violence. The Greek myth of Philomela tells of her rape by her brother-in-law Tereus, who mutilates her by cutting out her tongue to keep her from identifying him. Hundreds of years later, Toni Morrison's book *The Bluest Eye* tells the story of the twice-raped eleven-year-old Pecola, whose own father perpetrated one of the attacks. Tormented, ostracized, and disbelieved by her mother, Pecola loses her voice and, eventually, her mind.

When she was assaulted by Tereus, Philomela's loss of her voice kept her from speaking, but it didn't deprive her of the power to tell her story. She built a loom and wove a tapestry illustrating the details of the entire assault and had a servant deliver the tapestry to her sister, Procne, who immediately understood the story. Tereus was identified as the attacker, and Philomela was released from the shepherd's hut where she'd been held. Philomela's use of art to tell her story allowed her to defy the condition of silence, by reaching out to her sister, who helped her regain freedom.

Often the damage we suffer when we're silenced is more subtle, although still dangerous. Psychologist Carol Gilligan's study of silence in adolescent girls shows that if they began to hide what they knew or censored themselves, they developed psychological problems, such as eating disorders. Those who refused to be silenced were labeled as disruptive and worried that speaking up would harm their relationships.

By adulthood, we've internalized social norms about women's speech, making it hard for us to see silence as a form of oppression. We may deny we've been robbed of our voices, but the evidence shows up in the way we speak. How often have you re-worded your comments or softened your opinions to downplay what you knew to be true? How often have you begun a sentence with, "I could be wrong about this, but..."? We are socialized to speak with hesitancy, punished when we fail to defer to others, and rewarded when we follow social norms for women's speech. Across the years, we learn to become silent. We have been taught to dismiss or discount the stories told by our sisters of color and have, therefore, come to see our literary history as one grounded in the tales told about white women.

I strongly recommend that you set up your own **storying silence circle** with other women. Working with a group of supportive writers will allow you to hear pieces of your own stories in those told by others, and you'll feel safer as you navigate the emotions you're bound to encounter as you recover stories you've been afraid to tell. Collectively, we carry the seeds of unspoken tales of generations of women who have been unable to talk to one another about their lives. I suggest that deep listening is made the central goal of the writing group, as it has the potential to allow connections to develop. Learning to listen deeply to one another demands that we become aware of and release the fragility that has contributed to the decentering of stories carried by black women and allows us to learn from each other. At this time in our history, organizing a writing group has the potential to spark a movement to unsilence all women. In the words of social activist Grace Lee Boggs, these groups can inspire a "revolution that is based on the people exercising their creativity in the midst of devastation [and] is one of the greatest historical contributions of humankind." Remember, the stories you tell may be about your individual personal experiences, but as you write, you'll be lending energy to a creative revolution, one story at a time.

Your Call: Seeing Harsh Truths

Let's dive right into the work by identifying some difficult truths about the condition of silence and how it's imposed on us. We are surrounded by men's voices and stories of events interpreted by men, through the lens of a dominant white male narrative. We have normalized this way of telling the world's story to the point that we do not often recognize it, nor do we see how it contributes to our silencing.

Have you ever found yourself in any of the following situations?

- Being unable to finish making your point in a business meeting
- Being told by a friend (often by another woman) that you are responsible for fixing the relationship where you're being silenced
- Being advised to "leave" a situation where you've been discouraged from speaking up
- Being praised for your appearance when you're trying to be taken seriously about an issue
- Being told you are too intense, too angry, too _____
- Feeling bothered by books that indulge in stereotypical characterizations of women, especially women of color
- Feeling concerned about being honest with your doctor about how much pain you're in
- Being criticized for your deep emotions
- Having your tone policed
- Having a time limit placed on your so-called complaints
- Feeling exhausted by having to ask your spouse (just once more) to please take out the trash or another chore
- Feeling unseen in church because sermon messages involve stories about men or are only delivered by men (often by white men)
- Being corrected when you offer a fact or an opinion
- Being told you're too analytical, particular, or demanding
- Feeling restricted in the issues you're allowed to express anger about
- Being encouraged to express anger at other women, such as your mother, your co-worker, or a friend (a sexist way of pitting women against one another)
- Hearing a disparaging remark about a woman of color for being too loud, angry, or...
- Feeling that you have to explain yourself (more than you should)
- Being talked down to by anyone, including an insurance representative, a mechanic, or a store clerk
- Being asked to prove your point or offer evidence to support it

- Having your ideas or feelings trivialized
- Walking away from a discussion feeling as though you were not understood

These are all examples of being silenced. There are many more, but we often miss them because we're taught from childhood to let others control how and when we speak. By the time we reach adulthood, we've spent so many years being ignored, talked over, interrupted, corrected, or told to be quiet that we question whether or not we have a right to be heard. We live in a culture where silencing is reinforced by norms that value competition and domination. So, we often feel unheard, unseen, and invisible, and we may be carrying a deep anger–an unacknowledged rage–at this form of *injustice imposed by external forces.*

These days when I recall my talk, "The (Wo)man in the Mirror," I can more clearly see the outline of the person I was becoming: a story carrier who believes in the process of creating art (story) as a form of truth-telling. A woman who would no longer be denied the power of her own voice in public or private spaces. A woman who would not allow a dominant narrative to drown her voice. A woman who would forever defy attempts to shame her for feeling strong emotions. This is a life-long project, but it's one that allows me to see story carrying as a craft that will lead to the preservation of my sovereignty. As I put together the exercises in this workbook, it was with a vision of you, a woman capable of seeing how cultural attitudes and social norms discourage you from speaking up. A woman who can also write and speak in your own voice, who can name the forces that attempt to keep you under control by silencing you. A woman with the courage to see how she has failed to acknowledge the forces that have made it even more difficult for women of color to be heard and is willing to see this as a form of racism. A woman gifted with the power to weave together a story that unites other women in our journey to transform silence into a story of freedom. The woman I see in the reflection of this book is you. I wish you so much love as you move into your own deep forest of tales and discover the magic of your stories and their power to restore your voice.

Section 2:
Invocation

Engaging Your Voice

The following suggestions should help you prepare to write your responses and develop them into stories. Some will help you enter into a state of consciousness that will expand your ability to see how you've been silenced. Others will help you to step inside the story and experience it as it unfolds before your eyes. Still other suggestions will encourage you to stay the course when you become burdened by heavy emotions, or when you hit a metaphorical wall that seems to block you from thinking and writing. You may want to skim over these suggestions now and return to re-read them as you need to do so.

Ground Yourself
Create a Sanctuary for You and Your Story
Let Your Body Lead You to the Story It Wants to Tell
Drift Into Your Story
Treat Your Story as the Wave You'll Ride out of Silence
Use Your Story as a Portal to a Playground
Fool Around with Your Story
Don't be Afraid to let the Story Tell Itself
Listen for Untold Stories You are Carrying
Don't be Silenced by Overwhelm
Honor Your Story's Need for Privacy and Protection
See Yourself as a Member of a Bigger Storying Community
Treat Yourself as the Writing Warrior You are Becoming
Honor Your Story as Medicine
Write for the Sisterhood
A Final Note about Safety

Engaging
Your Voice

Ground Yourself

This is a good way to balance and orient yourself before you start writing. It is also good to pause and do it again during the writing, especially if you begin to feel shaky or unsafe. The suggestions here will help you keep your nervous system regulated, especially when painful memories surface.

Begin by sitting in a comfortable chair that supports your body. Straighten your spine and open up your chest (heart chakra). Become aware of your surroundings. This will engage your body's senses to let them know you are safe. Take a deep breath, feel your feet on the ground. Feel your seat on the chair or on a pillow on the floor. Lift your head up and notice what's above you. Return to the center and look across the room in front of you. Pause for a few seconds, then turn your head slowly to the right and notice what you see. Pause again. Turn your head slowly to the left and do the same thing. Then, gently turn around and look behind you, noticing what you see on the wall, on the floor.

Listen for any sounds you can hear. Take a second and notice the taste in your mouth. What do you smell? Place your hands over your heart and let them rest there for a full minute. Rub your hands up and down your arms gently. Wrap your arms around your shoulders and rock back and forth. Slowly.

Close your eyes and cover them with your hands. Your eyes work hard to take in information during the day. Let them sink back into their sockets and rest for a few seconds. You can gently massage the bones around your eyes and under your cheekbones. Open your eyes. You may also want to repeat this when you've finished writing to signal to your mind that you are now free to relax.

Some of the prompts in the book ask you to follow your imagination, allowing it to lead you to a deeper level of consciousness where you can experiment with unformed ideas or fragments of memories. This is where you catch pieces of your story, in the form of images, songs, smells, or feelings. Try to remember the things that come to you in this state. If you begin to feel uncomfortable, stop and ground yourself by re-orienting yourself.

NOTE: These are practices I've gathered from several sources and used across the years.

Create a Sanctuary for You and for Your Story

When you enter a space dedicated to healing, whether for a massage, a Reiki treatment, or a yoga session, you walk into a space that helps you open up to your senses. It may be filled with comfortable furnishings: cushions or pillows, plenty of sunlight or candlelight, soft music, sometimes crystals, plants, and other natural elements. The peaceful setting prepares you by telling your mind what to expect.

If you think of your writing as a practice that will lead to healing, you'll understand the importance of working in a safe space where you are surrounded by elements that help you relax and remain at peace as you work. Some writers have dedicated rooms or spaces which are free of outside interference, with limits on sound and boundaries for privacy. Your writing space should be treated as a destination where you'll be going to create a new world. The outside world–the one that's struggling with problems–should not be allowed to enter your space. I write on the third floor of my house in a room I have named "Haven," where, sitting at my desk, I can look out of the window across the field at the forest that borders my neighborhood. The walls are painted with a warm color that has tiny specks of glitter which seem to glimmer in the evening light, and soft, twinkling mini-lights line one of the walls. Along with a bookshelf filled with my favorite authors, I keep photographs and figurines of people who inspire me, including the ancestors I'm often writing about. This is my nest, my treatment room where I welcome stories and we begin our work together. You deserve a dedicated space where you can practice your creative healing. Fill it with your most precious possessions. Play background music (wordless is best). Use good lighting. This is your story sanctuary.

Let Your Body Lead You to the Story It Wants to Tell

Long ago I realized that I can't always trust my mind with a story because it may try to reason with me by telling me to move on or forget an experience. My body, however, is a signaling station that alerts me to the presence of a tale that my mind would prefer to push aside. Have you ever ignored a story so long that you began to have sensations in your body? An angry headache that wants you to scream about your boss's attitude toward you? A stomachache that calls you to slow down and breathe deeply so you can write the story of the loss of your best friend? When you "feel" a story in your body, you can ask what it wants to tell you. Go to the place where the feeling is strongest and begin to have a conversation, asking questions such as, "What are you saying to me, heart? Are you broken or heavy with grief?"

I once worked with an author who was struggling with writer's block that hit each time she tried to write about her early religious training in the Catholic Church. When I asked her to describe where the block landed in her body, she said it was in her throat and felt like a fish bone caught there. One evening, while writing a poem, she played with the image of the bone, and as she wrote, she remembered receiving a blessing to help cure a sore throat. In the poem, she wrote about the priest as a powerful figure in the church that had silenced her by placing strict rules on her ability to speak. Her body understood this as a form of silencing and by blocking her writing, it called her back to the sensation of the bone stuck in her throat. Following that feeling, she allowed her body to help her retrieve the story.

Sometimes, we have embodied reactions to our stories after we've written them. If you have physical symptoms after writing a response, ground yourself and begin to write about it. Trust the wisdom of your body to lead you.

Drift Into Your Story

In the song "Dance Me to the End of Love," Leonard Cohen's lyrics speak about the intimacy between lovers as a dance they perform. As he sings, he invites his partner to move him across the floor in a sweeping gesture that guides him with gentleness into loving abandonment. As a practice, writing is a performance that allows you, the writer, to engage intimately with the story, allowing it to move you in new ways, until you learn to surrender to its power. Your story is the dance, and as the writer, you are the dancer.

Before you begin to write, prepare your body for the work in much the same way a dancer prepares to move. Stretch, breathe, ground yourself. Practice somatic work (grounding or orienting) to bring your awareness to the present moment. This will help you center yourself, relax, and create a calm state of mind. Not only does this strengthen the connection between the physical and emotional self, but it also helps connect you to the rhythm of the tale, which allows you to glide gently across the fullness of the story.

Treat Your Story as The Wave You'll Ride Out of Silence

Story is an energy that exists in all beings, animating every aspect of our lives. Story travels across generations, dropping sparks of light onto the path of each life it crosses. It jumps across species, connecting human beings to the earth, through the stories shared between the trees of the forest, and those carried on the wings of winter geese that fly overhead. It travels on the breeze, moving across thresholds, carrying tales from our ancestors forward into our lives, settling itself like a seed into our bones. If you can learn to treat your story as a living energy, you can place yourself in its path and allow pieces of the story to fall into your soul and carry you into a new world that is not otherwise accessible to you.

Use Your Story as a Portal to a Playground

Remember your playground visits as a child? There were certain safety rules to follow, about who was allowed to climb the slide and who was allowed to use the swings. When your story calls to you to come and play, enter as though you're returning to that playground you remember from your childhood. Create a safe, sacred space to work. Watch out for strangers who seem not to belong–they may show up as inner critics who have no business in your space. Imagine yourself climbing to the top of the wooden castle where you can fight off dragons who want to steal your story from you. Think about putting your story on the seat of a wooden swing and pushing it up into the sky, where it can be free. While you're on the writing playground, stop writing long enough to lie on the grass and look for bugs and other critters who have crawled into your space.

Before you sit down to write, you might want to paint your story, make a collage, create a Play-Doh sculpture (this is always a hit in my writing workshops), crochet, knit, or sketch. Play music and dance, Tina Turner style. These practices will get you out of the logic-making area of your brain and move you deeper into the soul where so many good stories are lying in wait. Indulge in your writing as a performance. Dress up in a costume. Wear a pointy hat and write like a witch who is crafting a spell. Write in different genres, using different voices. Use a *nom de plume*. Be adventurous. Explore. Enjoy.

Fool Around with Your Story

Don't be shy with your story. Let it show you things you didn't know. Let it whisper secrets in your ear. Sing to your story. Ask your story what it wants to tell you. Dare it to be magical. As you write, think of your words as desires that want to be expressed.

Writing is cyclical and it tends to entice us into places we didn't know we could go. Allow yourself to follow its lead, moving back and forth across the page. Cut and paste words, moving them around until a new idea shows up. Let yourself fall in love with the story as it tells itself and return to it again and again, searching for something you may have missed.

An interesting way to play with your stories/responses is to write several versions of the same response, then print them out and lay them on the floor, beside one another. You may notice the energy moving between stories, almost as if they feel a connection or to each other. Trust this as a sign that the story may have more layers to it than you know.

As you write, you may discover some stories that overlap what you've written in another one. Follow the trail from one to the other and be prepared to be surprised by what you learn as you write. The story often knows more than the writer so allow yourself to listen deeply.

Don't Be Afraid to Let the Story Tell Itself

You are in a partnership with your story, and you'll need to navigate your relationship as you work. Like any good relationship, you'll need to listen and learn to move out of the way to allow the story to unfold. Listen even when it brings you to difficult memories. You may not find the words to express your feelings. You might even feel overwhelmed and stop yourself from writing. Although some refer to this as writer's block, I see it as an important signal, telling you that you've touched on a deeper, more important story that wants to be told. Try to relax into the experience. Narrative writing causes us to remember and re-feel the emotions associated with the original event. When you write about being silenced, you may feel the original sense of shame and embarrassment. Your body will remember how you felt and will replay the sensations, so it feels like you are re-living the experience. Be compassionate with yourself. This is your testimony as a survivor. Try not to censor or question yourself if you feel anger, rage, even despair or hopelessness. Everything you feel is part of the story. Keep everything.

Listen for Untold Stories You are Carrying

It's helpful to know that you may be carrying untold stories that have been passed down by ancestors for several generations. Psychiatrist Galit Atlas writes that stories–even those we've **never** heard–are absorbed into our DNA, where they are transmitted by a genetic template, much like the traits of hair and eye color. These untold stories will "haunt us like ghosts," says Dr. Atlas. You may feel the presence of an ancestor sitting with you as you write. Please know that this is common, and it does not mean you've done something wrong. It means you've fully opened yourself up to the power of story. This happened to me as I wrote about my ancestral line and in allowing myself to tune into the story, I discovered fascinating, powerful stories that were hidden in my family. Trust yourself when–and if–you feel haunted by a story that has no words.

Don't Be Silenced by Overwhelm

This is noble work you are doing–both for yourself and for those who will someday read your stories. You're telling truths that others may not want to be told. It's said that when the messenger arrives, the truth is told, and you have been chosen as a messenger. You may experience conflicted feelings about your work, and I suggest making a plan to handle them as they come up.

If you begin to feel guilt or any negative feelings as you write, you may also give yourself a context for your feelings by writing a list of the experiences that have brought you joy, the things you love, the places you have been. This will keep you on track by reminding you of your mission to story your life. Working with difficult stories opens up new opportunities to make sense or meaning out of our experiences.

Camus said about this dynamic, "Those are clarifying times, sanctifying times, when the simulacra of meaning we have consciously and unconsciously borrowed from our culture…fall away to reveal the naked soul of being, to hone the spirit of the moral bone."

If you find yourself cycling through dramatic highs and lows as you write, giving yourself space to rest between the peaks and valleys will allow new insights and ideas to appear. Take advantage of these quiet, peaceful spaces as times of asylum where you recover before returning to the story.

Remember that you are bringing pain to the surface where you can work with it in a creative way. Your story of suffering also holds pieces of a tale yet to be seen, treasures hidden from the naked eye. If you are writing about something very difficult, even traumatic, set a timer and limit your exposure to the memory to a few minutes at a time.

If at any point you begin to feel engulfed by strong feelings that you can't overcome, do not hesitate to reach out for support, either from friends who are safe or with a trauma-informed professional. I recommend working with a non-traditional therapist who does not treat your stories as symptoms of a pathology, but sees you as a complex human being who is struggling to carry the collective stories of a world in a global crisis. A world that has silenced women. (Read more about this in the section on mental health).

Honor Your Story's Need for Privacy and Protection

I strongly suggest that you do not share your work until you feel safe. Sharing an early draft may leave you feeling exposed and more vulnerable. Do not let a spouse, companion, or your children read your early drafts. Your story may not align with the reality they are carrying (in fact, it most likely will not) and sharing yours may put you in a position where you'll feel defensive. While you're protecting your work, allow yourself to experience a sense of possessiveness and jealousy of your creativity. This is natural. You're falling in love with your beautiful story, so treat it as a coveted treasure.

See Yourself (and Your Story) as a Member of a Bigger Storying Community

Remind yourself that you are not alone. Your story is what connects you to other women. Therapist Martha Crawford explains, "Whenever we can identify parts of our identities or stories that have been erased, isolated, or suppressed, we are often identifying shared experiences that the larger culture does not support." As you disclose your experience, you are drawing an invisible line that ties you to other women who also have been silenced. You might want to sketch this as an image you can return to when you need to be reminded that your work is restorative for other women. This can also be a powerful concept to use for creating a collage.

Treat Yourself as the Writing Warrior You are Becoming

Roar! You are a goddess, a midwife. You are embracing your sacred feelings, birthing a new story or the re-telling of an old one. You are stepping away from the passive role of being silenced into that of a creator who is storying her silence. Reward yourself for your courage and dedication to this work. Writing about personal (difficult) experiences is an experiential process and it will call on your body, mind, and soul. This is a kind of writing that is as athletic as it is creative or intellectual, and it demands as much stamina and strength as someone training for a marathon. Reward yourself for having the courage to begin the work and to withstand the discomfort. Take breaks. Buy yourself a bouquet of tulips, take a walk in the woods, fix a special flavor of coffee, or brew a steaming cup of herbal tea. Take lots of naps during the day. Do some grounding work after you've written. Take care of the warrior author you are becoming.

Honor Your Story as Medicine

Your story is your medicine. Your resistance. Your willingness to step into this process speaks of your readiness to accept your story as an initiation into a sometimes raw and deep meeting with strong feelings. It signals to your body to release those stories you've carried in your bones, in your blood, and your womb, allowing them to rise up and begin to transform you. As a story carrier, know that you have never been alone on this journey. You have been accompanied by ancestors–mothers, aunts, and grandmothers–who also carried medicine. You will be writing during one of the most important historic periods of our lifetime. Your stories will raise your awareness of others' stories carried in the collective unconscious, such as those of women living in war-torn nations, women who suffer acts of violence, and even stories carried by non-speaking beings who share this planet with us. Allow yourself to feel the restorative power of being connected to those stories. Be aware that the entire world is telling a story. Reach out with your heart. This is an antidote to isolation and hopelessness many of us are now experiencing.

Write for the Sisterhood

While we are surrounded by men's stories, told about men and by men, our lives are portrayed in the lyrics of songwriters such as Taylor Swift, whose autobiographical works are described by NPR's Ann Powers as a "sword of justice," penned and performed in the style of "women saints who smote abusive fathers and priests in the name of an early Christian Jesus."

But to fully expand our work, I am also recommending that we come to terms with the fact that many of the stories we read and write are focused on predominantly white women's heteronormative experiences. Many portray white women as victims in a dangerous world. Part of reclaiming our autonomy requires that we not only resist this characterization and expand beyond our levels of comfort and listen deeply to the stories carried by women from other groups, including those who have been marginalized. Even if we never have the opportunity to write alongside a woman from a marginalized group who is writing to unsilence herself, we need to acknowledge that for some, the experience of oppression is compounded by other factors, such as racism and, perhaps by social class. Writing for the sisterhood means beginning to witness the stories carried by all women. It means that we must make space to include the stories of women who have been oppressed in multiple ways. We can no longer see ourselves as fragile, voiceless women.

Your story is your legend. Your myth. It's more than a what-happened-to-me tale. It's herstory. Imagine even a small piece of your story being read in the future by a young girl who is curious about the lives of women who lived during the erosion of constitutional rights. Writing your story is not only a way of storying your way out of silence, it's a way of establishing permanence. In the words of author Jeannine Ouellette, "Our art is proof that we are still here. The stories we tell, the images we shape, the songs we raise–these are the bridges we build between one another, the threads that keep us from unraveling."

A Final Note About Safety

The writing prompts I have offered are meant to help you come to terms with your personal response to the systems that have imposed silence on you. As you write, you may, at times, feel powerful emotions that frighten you. This is a natural response. You are being asked to see what you may have been taught to ignore, and it can be confusing and disorienting. You may feel a sense of betrayal by the culture that has taken your voice. A trusted friend or a supportive writing group is the best way to help you navigate tumultuous feelings. By sharing your writing experience, you might help another woman identify her own silencing. Again, you may choose to work with a trauma-informed professional–specifically, one who is trained to listen deeply for stories without using the material to pathologize you. We all have very strong feelings about being oppressed, but none of your responses should be used to diagnose you. This can feel like another method of controlling your voice. Safety is the most important element anytime you share, so be very kind to your story and to yourself. If at any time you begin to feel unsafe or stuck in feelings that are too difficult to navigate, take steps to reach out for support.

Section 3:
Initiation

Stepping Out of Silence

Childhood Experiences
Personal Adult Relationships
Abusive Relationships
Rape/Gender Violence
The Body and Beauty Standards
Health and Medical Conditions
Reproductive Health
Motherhood, Being Mothered, Caretaking
Adoption
Mental Health
Ancestral Stories
Workplace Experiences of Harassment and Discrimination
Home (as a Worksite)
Spiritual Spaces
Grief

Stepping Out
of Silence

Each part of this section opens with a brief excerpt from a story that is either told about women or by women. Some show how our stories have been appropriated by others or have been subsumed under a dominant narrative that casts women in supporting, minor roles. These sections will help you come to terms with the complex ways in which stories told about women are used to diminish and silence us. Others will illustrate how women have taken back narrative control over their lives by telling their own stories, even in the face of danger. As you read these tales, imagine seeing yourself in the story.

The excerpts are followed by prompts asking you to write your story. Allow yourself to write for 15-20 minutes without stopping to correct or edit your work. Tell what happened, how you felt about the situation, how you responded, what sort of reaction you got, and how you feel about the experience now. Add details as they come to you. *If you catch yourself editing too much, understand that you may be silencing yourself.*

After you've finished, let your **initial response** sit for a few hours or a few days to metabolize or begin to "cook." The story will remain with you, in your mind, in your soul. The thing about writing stories is we never stop working on them; once we begin to write, the story will pick us up and lead us into a generative, intimate space where we can explore new ways of seeing and understanding our experiences. As your story leads you, you may begin to see it and your life in quite different ways.

Childhood Experiences

NOTE: The prompts in this area are focused on childhood experiences and they are intended to help you explore some of the key events of your early life. **You will do more than write in this section; you'll dig up bones and I can promise you it will leave you feeling a bit shaky and in need of support, so reach out if you need to do so.**

Did you read *The Tale of Peter Rabbit* as a child, or have you read it to your children? When Beatrix Potter wrote this classic children's story, about the mischievous bunny who ignored his mother's warnings and was almost killed for raiding Mr. McGregor's garden, she gave it to her governess's son who was suffering with scarlet fever. As the story goes, Beatrix captured, suffocated, and stuffed the little rabbit she drew to illustrate the book. If that seems odd, knowing something about her childhood and early life will help you understand how she viewed herself as a unique writer of children's books. Beatrix grew up in a wealthy family with parents who were strict disciplinarians, in a home she called a prison. As a young scientist, she was ridiculed and her research on fungus rejected by London's Linnean Society even though it was later found to be both accurate and valuable. Controlled as a child and silenced as a woman, Potter and her protagonist, Peter, became symbols of rebellion who wandered away from the proverbial garden owned by men.

In this section, you'll find prompts asking you to write about your childhood experiences. You may be reluctant to do so, either because you were told not to, or because you don't fully trust your memories but, like Beatrix Potter, your early experiences were recorded in a story that will emerge at some time in your life. You may barely remember the details of an event because you haven't stored them in your long-term memory, but your body has not forgotten. As you write, allow yourself to open up to unformed memories you've carried across your lifetime.

Sisterly Guidance

Writing reactivates neurons in the brain, reviving a piece or pieces of the memory, stirring feelings that may make you feel untethered. You may experience more trauma as you write and even have physical symptoms, such as sleep disturbances, stomach aches, headaches, muscle tightness, or feelings of panic. You may even feel numb and begin to dissociate. Use the grounding (orienting) exercises to bring your nervous system back into regulation. If at any point you become overwhelmed or stuck in your feelings, reach out for support from a trauma-informed therapist.

Writing Prompts for Stories of Childhood Experiences

1. Write a story about a time you felt abandoned as a child. You may not have a fully developed memory of the event, but you may be able to recall enough to string together pieces of a story. This could be a significant loss of a relative, a friend, or a pet. Were you encouraged to remember this experience? If so, tell how. If not, explain how this affected you.

2.

Write about a time when a friend or family member betrayed you.

3.   Write about a time when you felt you were unloved.

Additional Thoughts

- Deep breathing, meditation, or yoga may help you as you work.

- Feelings may feel tangled together when you begin to write, and you'll want to try to separate your feelings *about the experience* from the feelings caused by *being told not to speak about it.* Everything matters so keep everything you write.

- You may need a plan to rescue yourself from the return of intense emotions. Talk with a therapist or join a support group. Be very gentle with yourself. If the entire story is too frightening or you begin to have symptoms of dissociation, stop and seek support from a non-traditional therapist, spiritual director, or a trusted friend.

- Sometimes it's easier to tell the story in pieces, using a clock to control the amount of time you spend writing. Take good care of yourself. Reward yourself. Get extra sleep.

- Kaori Ikeda and Hayley Teasdale write that even when a child cannot recall specific events, a "latent trace of the memory of early experience remains for a long period of time and can be triggered by a later reminder." A smell, sound, or an image can bring up a memory that is not attached to a fully-formed thought.

- Unable to start writing? Try this:

- Try somatic writing by using physical sensations as entryways into emotions and memories.

- It's not necessary to write in full paragraphs or sentences. Simply allow words to come up and try to attach them to feelings. Let yourself write freely until you find the words that fit. Write in any order. Allow the words to marinate and return to them in a few hours or a few days to see what story they are trying to tell you. Add new words and details as they come to you.

- Make a collage of your feelings and memories. Do not try to follow a plot or storyline as you make your collage; simply pick out pictures that call to you and allow them to direct you as you arrange them into a picture. Again, allow the images to metabolize. Then, write.

Personal Adult Relationships

We've all heard the stories included in the collection of Middle Eastern folktales known as the *Arabian Nights*, or *1001 Nights,* such as "Sinbad the Sailor," and "Aladdin," but did you know they came from a set of tales told by a young Persian princess who used storytelling to save her life? Sometime in the 9th century, Princess Scheherazade was given in marriage to a king who, out of jealousy, brutally beheaded several of his previous wives. Every day, he married another woman and beheaded her the next morning, before she could dishonor him. When she married him, Scheherazade made a plan to save herself from the same fate by using her gift for stories to keep her husband entertained. Each night, she began to tell the king a story, leaving it incomplete with a promise to finish it the next night. He was so enchanted by the tales that he put off her execution for 1001 nights and eventually spared her life. Not many women have marriages or relationships this challenging, but it's true that many of us carry the burden of managing the emotional labor of maintaining our relationships and we can lose track of our own needs in the process. We can lose sight of ourselves.

The following prompts ask you to consider your intimate relationships. These prompts can be applied to any adult relationship, regardless of how you define yours. They should help you become aware of how you use your voice to navigate your relationships.

Sisterly Guidance

Be prepared for big feelings to surface as you write. They will and you'll want to be prepared. Do not share your responses with anyone, particularly not with your significant other. Give yourself time to metabolize your feelings because they may change over time as you write. Do not allow anyone to pathologize or label your feelings.

Writing Prompts for Stories About Personal Adult Relationships

1. Write a story about a difficult romantic relationship you've experienced, including as much detail as you remember. If you ended the relationship, tell how you did so and how it affected you.

2.

Write as much as you know about difficult marriages and/or romantic relationships of other women in your family, including divorces, deaths, betrayals, and abuse. What, if anything, were you told about these relationships and how do you think they influenced your own?

3. If you or your parents were divorced (or you are going through a divorce), write a story about it. What were you taught about divorce? Did your family's expectations or those of your religious community influence your feelings?

4. Write about a time when you experienced the same lessons through more than one relationship or experience. Try to avoid judging yourself as you write, avoiding terms such as "codependent." (This is a form of self-silencing.)

5. Make a list of the small (and large) ways you maintain your current relationship. Make one for your partner.

Additional Thoughts

The importance of Scheherazade's framing narrative is often overlooked by critics who focus on the individual stories she told, which are focused on the lives of men. How do you think she might have told her story if she'd had control over the narrative?

Abusive Relationships

Joan of Arc's story, about her deadly ordeal with the Catholic Church that tried her on charges of heresy and executed her, was told through the official court transcripts of her trial. Five hundred years later, the Church revised her story, telling about St. Joan, the divine military leader responsible for France's victory over the English. A few years afterward, Mark Twain wrote about Joan, glorifying her and elevating her to near-angelic status. But the story of the complex, wise young woman, led by divine visions, was never told by Joan in her own words. Much like Joan's, the stories told by women seeking legal protection from violent relationships are seldom told in their own words. Their stories are considered to be dangerous because they threaten to expose the existence of attitudes of supremacy and reveal domestic violence as a social problem. When they turn to the system for help, their accounts are collapsed onto the pages of official police reports and court records. Their voices are drowned by legal reporting requirements that downplay their suffering in language that portrays violence as an intimate partner problem. This characterization further victimizes women by removing their narrative control. As the experience is written up in legal terms, the story of the woman may disappear.

One in three women around the world will experience domestic violence, and the danger is higher for women of color. The Bureau of Justice Statistics reports that Black women experience intimate partner violence at a rate 35% higher than white women. One in three Latinas and 48% of Native American and Alaska Native women will experience violence, while 21-55% of Asian women will endure intimate partner violence. Yet, these women are less likely to report the abuse, probably because they are not well served by a system filled with racism.

If you have survived an abusive relationship or are working to free yourself from one, writing your story in your own words is a way to preserve your truth. In telling your story, you are refusing to give the abuser your silence. You are speaking up against a system that may be uncomfortable with your experience and will try to diminish it. While writing your story does not erase the harm you have suffered, it is a form of resistance to a society that would prefer not to know the truth you are telling about the prevalence of violence in our world.

Sisterly Guidance

In my work with survivors of domestic violence, I discovered the need to tell the story multiple times, over a period of time. Do not become discouraged if you need to do this. Also, do not feel that telling your story to a therapist or counselor obligates you to take any action. Sometimes, simply being able to tell the story is all we can do. Telling it is a way of restoring control and autonomy.

Writing Prompts for Stories About Abusive Relationships

1. Write about an experience where a partner was physically violent with you. Include as many details as you can recall. Return to your draft to add additional details as they come to you.

2. Write about a time when a partner made hurtful, insulting, or threatening remarks to you. Include as many details as you can remember.

3. Write about a time when you confronted a partner about his/her hurtful behavior, and he/she denied it or blamed you.

4. If your mother, sister, grandmother, or other female relatives experienced violence or abusive treatment from a partner, write about it.

5. Make a list of the feelings you have experienced about your relationship. Keep the details to yourself or share with another woman who is comfortable with your honesty. My experience as a legal advocate for survivors of domestic violence made me aware of the intolerance in the legal system for the intense feelings of women who have been violated. Some legal professionals may use this discomfort as justification to ignore your danger.

6. If you sought relief from the police or the courts, write about your experience. Did you find it to be helpful? Did you feel silenced in any way? Did you find support from family or friends as you pursued justice?

Important Note

If you are in an abusive relationship, make a plan to keep yourself safe as you write. Do not leave anything you've written in a public place. I recommend saving it on a USB that's portable and keeping it in a safe location. The National Domestic Violence Hotline also warns that internet browser history and computer use may be monitored by an abusive partner, saying "Internet usage...is impossible to erase completely. If you're concerned your internet usage might be monitored, call us at 800.799.SAFE (7233)." Trust your instincts here. Seek outside help from a trained professional, preferably a domestic violence counselor. Some women agree to attend marriage counseling with abusive husbands or partners, but, as a former counselor, I strongly advise against doing so. It will be safer for you to consult your own advocate for help.

Additional Facts

- One in three women around the world will experience violence from an intimate partner at some point in their lifetime.
- 80 percent of the casualties of the ongoing wars around the world are women and children.
- A long-term additional effect of abuse is silencing imposed on women by a system that frightens and shames us. This form of gaslighting can lead women to internalize the message that we are not worthy of protection.
- Women of color experience domestic violence at much higher rates than white women. They are also more likely to be killed by intimate partners. Black women comprise 8% of the U.S. population but account for 22% of partner homicides, according to the Bureau of Justice Statistics.

Additional Thoughts

- Whether or not you are in an abusive relationship, know that we are all changed by violent acts perpetrated against our sisters and we are all touched by the existence of attitudes of white supremacy that allow such violence to occur.
- When our stories become the instruments of institutions, they are often weakened, and our voices are removed.

Rape/Gender Violence

As I was writing this book, Gisele Pelicot spoke out in a courtroom in Mazan, France about her husband who drugged her and the more than 50 men who raped her while she was incapacitated. Pelicot's voice rang across the room as she told her story, refusing to be silenced by accepting the shame usually imposed on assault victims. In her trial testimony, Pelicot said she spoke up because she "wanted all women who are rape victims to say to themselves, 'Mrs. Pelicot did it, so we can do it too.' It's not us who should feel shame, but [the perpetrators]."

The case ripped off the cover of the hidden problem of rape culture in France, where in 2023, 114,000 victims of sexual violence were reported according to authorities. The numbers are not better in the United States, where the National Sexual Violence Resource Center estimates that 1 in 5 women will be raped, and half of those experience rape by an intimate partner.

Gender violence is a symptom of white male supremacy and it affects more women of color, who live at the intersection of harm caused by racism, sexism, and other forms of discrimination. According to the US Department of Justice, 44% of lesbian women and 61% of bisexual women have been victims of rape or physical violence, while more than half of American Indian and Alaska Native women have suffered sexual violence at some point in their lives.

The majority of us have experienced some form of aggression that has fallen just short of rape. These are assaults against our physical, emotional, and instinctive natures, and not one of us is exempt from the way they tear at our sense of safety. Unfortunately, current political conditions have exacerbated rape culture in America, making it more important than ever to write about the stress it is causing for all women. Our silence, while understandable, contributes to the ideology that allows rape culture to exist and may reduce our ability to see ourselves in this environment.

Sisterly Guidance

This is a very difficult form of violence to come to terms with, and it's important to have the right kind of support as you write your story. Black women often encounter more resistance when they report gender violence, such as worse access to medical, legal, and psychological services. They are also judged by stereotypical notions about women and sexuality and sometimes judged to be responsible for their own abuse. If you need support, you can find a counselor or advocate through the National Sexual Violence Resource Center or through a center in your local area. It may be too difficult to share your story with anyone in your intimate circle, so use your judgment about doing so. Gender violence is all about robbing control of your body and your voice; writing, while difficult in the beginning, is meant to help restore your voice and give you some sense of control again. Deciding when and how to share your story is another way to assert control. Trust your instincts and know that you have the right to remain silent if you choose to do so. Try not to let anyone shame you or talk you out of your feelings of outrage and fear. Know that your story is important!!!

Writing Prompts for Stories About Rape or Sexual Violence

1. Write your rape/sexual abuse story. (Keep yourself in a safe place while writing). I recommend working with a rape counselor or a trauma-informed therapist. And I strongly suggest you work with a woman.

2. Write about an experience where you were directly threatened or felt threatened with sexual violence. This includes both in-person threats and online hostility that made you feel afraid for your safety.

3. Write a story about the way living in a rape culture feels to you. For example, does it require you to avoid working out in certain locations? Do you avoid certain areas where you feel unsafe? If you have trouble finding the language to describe this, read what has been written about the effect of male supremacy on gender violence by the Institute for Research on Male Supremacism (theirms.org/what-is-male-supremacism).

4. If you have sought protection in the justice system, write a story about your experience. Your story will contribute to an important history about the way women are treated by the system.

5.

Write a story about the small (and large) steps you have taken to reclaim your own safety. Or, write about the way you silence yourself about living in rape culture. For example, do you discuss it openly with your friends or your daughter?

Important

If you have been a victim of a sexual assault, you can contact the National Sexual Assault Hotline 24/7 number at 800-656-HOPE (4673). Or you can chat with them at online.rainn. org. Regardless of whether you decide to report your assault, it is helpful to keep an account of the precise details of what you experienced and to protect your information by making a copy and keeping it in a safe location. Writing about this will be very difficult but could also be a beginning to restoring your sense of autonomy.

Additional Facts

- Rape is the most underreported crime so tracking is difficult, but the United Nations says 15 million young women (between the ages of 15-19) will experience forced sex in their lifetime.

- According to UN Women, reporting is influenced by the presence of rape culture, which is the "social environment that allows sexual violence to be normalized and justified, fueled by the persistent gender inequalities and attitudes about gender and sexuality."

- In her book, *Down Girl: The Logic of Misogyny,* Kate Manne describes the pressure we face to remain silent about gender-based violence as a form of misogyny, which is "primarily about controlling, policing, punishing, and exiling the 'bad' women who challenge male dominance. And it's compatible with rewarding 'the good ones,' and singling out other women to serve as warnings to those who are out of order."

- Rape and gender violence are crimes of power and they are enacted when one person (or more) with power uses violence against another one. According to the Rape Abuse and Incest National Network (RAINN) an American is assaulted every 68 seconds and every 9 minutes that person is a child.

The Body and Beauty Standards

Have you read "The Birthmark," the story about the young scientist Aylmer who is so obsessed with a small mark on his wife Georgiana's cheek that he talks her into letting him remove it? When Georgiana gives in, allowing her husband to use a chemical mixture to make the mark disappear, he is ecstatic. But his joy is cut short when Georgiana tells him that she is dying, and the birthmark was the only thing that has kept her divine spirit connected to her human body. This 1843 story, written by Nathaniel Hawthorne (yes, the one who wrote *The Scarlet Letter*) may sound like a fantastic cautionary tale about a mad scientist's hubris, but it's also a story about a woman who is pressured into allowing herself to be erased.

We live in a world that objectifies women, turning us into sexual instruments and we're overwhelmed with media messages about our appearance. Social media has become a gateway for women to enter into the performance arena by adopting traditional gender norms and displaying feminine ideals of purity and beauty. The socialization of women is so subtle and seems so harmless on the surface, it's often not recognized. However, hidden beneath the surface is the notion of a preferred appearance based on white European femininity, which excludes those who do not fit this image. Objectification is a way of excluding some women and making all of us disappear, much like Aylmer did to Georgiana.

Women are often judged on their bodies by a health industry that tells us that we can control our own health and that it is in fact our personal responsibility to do so. This becomes a bigger danger when we conflate health with the pursuit of thinness as a moral standard, following beauty and health trends that promise unattainable physical standards.

The prompts in this section are not meant to judge women who've opted to have cosmetic correction or work to maintain fitness or a certain body size. Instead, they are meant to help you become aware of the messages that pressure women to live up to a demand imposed on us by a culture obsessed with beauty.

Sisterly Guidance

Be very gentle with yourself. Share your work with a trusted friend or group of women. Talk about your feelings with your daughters, your husband, your sons.

Writing Prompts on the Body and Beauty Standards

1. Write about the pressure you've felt trying to meet unrealistic beauty standards. Can you see yourself in the story, "The Birthmark"?

2. Write about a time when you were the target of body shaming for being too much: too tall, too short, too thin, too fat. Who shamed you? How did it make you feel?

3. Write about the way you learned about how to take care of your body. What kind of information do you now feel you need to care for your body?

4. Write about how you maintain fitness. Do you spend time in a gym or working out? What is your main reason for doing so? How do you feel about the pressure to maintain fitness?

5. Write about the conditions that are beyond your control which impact your fitness. For example, do you have diabetes? Did you inherit a body shape/size from your family?

Additional Thoughts

- When we pursue beauty at the expense of health, we can become vulnerable to conditions such as asthma, early menstruation, and, even to cancer, writes Karen Feldscher of the Harvard T.H. Chan School of Public Health.

- Even women who do meet the narrow definition of beauty in this culture aren't free from pressure. As a commodity that grants "pretty privilege," or unearned benefits to some, beauty can be used to pit women against one another.

- As far as we've come, women are still subjected to what Dr. Valerie Rein describes as an "accepted cultural entitlement to body judgment" that keeps us engaged in self-monitoring and criticism, leaving us unable to connect to our bodies in healthy ways.

Health and Medical Conditions

Years ago, I attended a Narrative Medicine Conference led by Dr. Rita Charon, head of the Narrative Medicine Department at Columbia University, who introduced the idea of illness as a story wanting to be told. Dr. Charon trained medical students in the practice of deep listening to patients' stories and combined the details with results of clinical lab tests to allow the two sources of information to tell a more layered, complete tale that took in all aspects of patients' lives. The process allowed the patient to be seen. After years of facilitating writing groups, I have come to believe all stories are embodied–whether about illness or health–and when we're unable to tell them, our health and even our lifespan is threatened.

Consider that 80 percent of those who suffer from autoimmune diseases and other chronic illnesses are women, who doctors believe are predisposed to these conditions by the very same qualities that make it possible to silence us. Sadly, this may be overlooked by a medical model that doesn't fully appreciate the body/mind connection. This can lead to medical gaslighting, when a health care provider dismisses, trivializes, or undermines your symptoms, feelings, or concerns about your health.

Racism is still a problem in medicine, where an institution charged with protecting the health of patients may dismiss, ignore, or blame the patient for their suffering. This form of gaslighting is a serious concern for BIPOC and may extend harm to patients already at risk of racism by delaying diagnoses and leading to disparities in treatment.

Whether you received inadequate medical care, or felt you were not seen and heard by your physician, your feelings are valid, and you should treat them as signals that you deserve better. In this section, you are asked to write about any interactions or experiences with a medical professional that have left you feeling uncomfortable. This could be lifesaving stuff, so don't forget any of the details.

Sisterly Guidance

Be very gentle with yourself. If the entire story is triggering, write about that. Identify which part has triggered you and the memories it brings up for you. If you begin to have symptoms of dissociation, stop and seek support. When you return to the story, tell it in pieces, using a timer to control the amount of time you spend writing. Ground yourself in the present by following the exercises in Section 2 ("Ground Yourself"). Take good care of yourself. Seek out support from a therapist, spiritual director, or close friend. Keep in mind that the story you write may contribute to future research on women's health.

Writing Prompts for Stories About Health and Medical Conditions

1. Write the story of your illness: the whole story, including how you live, who cares for you, how your illness has impacted your life and the lives of your intimate others.

2. Write a story about a time when you got inadequate medical care.

3. Write about a time when a doctor either used a placebo to treat you or downplayed your symptoms.

4. Write about a time when your doctor did not encourage you to expect a good outcome and good health. Tell how this felt.

5. Write a story about a medical treatment that traumatized you. These are such important stories and very few people write them. In fact, much of the treatment we receive traumatizes us, whether it's from a dentist who's working in an intimate zone (mouth), or a doctor who is too rough or simply when treatment causes more pain. This kind of trauma is cumulative so expect heavy feelings to come to the surface as you write!

6. If you are a person of color, write about a time when your doctor downplayed your pain or assumed you were able to tolerate more pain.

Important

If you are in a hospital and your care is not good, you may reach out to the hospital ombudsman. If you are a Medicare recipient, you may seek help through an ombudsman at 1-800-MEDICARE (1-800-633-4227).

Additional Thoughts

- Physical discomfort has become the norm for women. Dr. Valerie Rein writes, "Feeling unsafe inside our own bodies is a woman's baseline. As a result, our nervous systems stay in a high level of activation–which translates into chronic stress and chronic illness." Fear of being seen as overly dramatic or not wanting to be seen as demanding may make us reluctant to speak assertively to our doctors.

- Your treatment may be influenced by a model called the biopsychosocial model, which has been criticized for blaming chronic pain on a "broken alarm system" that rules a patient's mind and nervous system. In this model, "catastrophizing thoughts and avoidant behaviors are not byproducts of unresolved pain, but rather the causes of ongoing suffering," writes Carli Cutchin. Researcher Joanne Hunt, of Department of Women's and Children's Health at Uppsala University in Sweden, decries this model as a form of "victim-blaming, gaslighting...which places responsibility for 'recovery'" on the sufferer.

- Unfortunately, medical gaslighting results in harmful effects on patients, some of whom are emotionally manipulated by the medical professionals tasked to care for them. This is especially true for "invisible" illnesses, which may be difficult to diagnose. A recent survey conducted by SheKnows revealed that 72 percent of women felt they were a victim of medical gaslighting.

- Understanding the troubling history of medicine with that of slavery in America is important. In the mid-1800s, Dr. James Marion Sims conducted experimental medical treatment on enslaved Black women and girls who could not consent.

Reproductive Health

The story of women gathering to support women during menstruation and childbirth is the center of the book *The Red Tent* by Anita Diamant. The story is about Dinah, the daughter of Jacob and Leah, and it traces the refuge she creates in the desert for the women of Jacob's tribe. Dinah's story has become a beacon, not only because it gives voice to a Hebrew woman who is all but silenced in the book of Genesis, but because it also celebrates women's reproductive gifts. The story offers a history of health care practiced by women before the invention of the birth control pill, when more natural methods were used to prevent pregnancy.

We are at a moment in history when gathering in circles to tell our stories of reproductive health can unite us against efforts to silence us. As more states adopt laws that criminalize our wombs, our voices are being discounted. We are increasingly ignored by a legal system that has defined the debate as an argument of morality, which limits the stories we can tell as either "pro" or "anti" abortion/life. This blocks us from having a more meaningful, nuanced dialogue, and allows those in control to pit women against one another. We cannot allow for this sophisticated, legal tactic to silence women to go unchecked; we must redefine the ground rules of the debate. By writing and sharing stories about our reproductive health, we collectively respond to attempts to "control women according to our reproductive potential," according to Sarah Petersen.

When women of color write stories about their reproductive history, more chapters are added to the historical record filled with tales about the cruel medical experiments that began during slavery and continued with the forced sterilization of young girls in Mississippi and the southern states. Your story can raise the awareness of discrimination that still exists in reproductive health care.

Sisterly Guidance

Be very gentle with yourself. If you do not have answers, reach out to a good gynecologist and ask her about ways to educate yourself. The field has advanced significantly in the last twenty years and much more information is available. Writing your own story about your reproductive health will contribute to the collective narrative and add momentum to the demand for ongoing research.

Writing Prompts About Reproductive Health

1. Write a story about your reproductive health history.

2.

Write about your reproductive health care.

3.

Write a piece about your opinion in the debate over reproductive rights.

4. Write a short (or long) piece about your experience with menopause. When did you become aware of having pre-menopausal symptoms? When did you enter menopause? Did you have good medical care? Do you still have questions about the experience? If you have not yet reached this stage in life, what do you look forward to or fear about it? Do you feel your physician has helped you to prepare for this experience?

5. Write a story about your mother's experience with reproductive health and/or menopause. If your mother is still living, treat this as an opportunity to build a connection with her and give her the encouragement to unsilence herself about this health experience.

Additional Thoughts

- **Maternal Health Care.** Let's be clear about maternal health care in the United States. It is not good. According to the World Health Organization, 800 women die from preventable complications related to pregnancy and childbirth every year. Between 2020 and 2021, the Centers for Disease Control and Prevention reported a 40% increase in maternal deaths, rising from 861 to 1,205. The rate was more than 2 ½ times higher for women of color. Women of color are 3 to 4 times more likely to die from complications of childbirth, according to the World Health Organization.

- **Menopause.** There is an emerging movement to educate women about menopause, which will affect EVERY woman in the world. Now that millennials are entering menopause, women have begun to drive the conversation, and doctors are beginning to both specialize in menopause medicine and educate our sisters about the importance of care.

- Dr. Karen Tang writes, "Reproductive health care, from abortion to gender-affirming care, is under siege." In her book, *It's Not Hysteria,* Tang says, "Ninety percent of women experience menstrual abnormalities or pelvic issues in their lifetime. Yet these conditions are overwhelmingly misunderstood, misdiagnosed, or dismissed. The root causes for these issues, such as PCOS, endometriosis, fibroids, ovarian cysts, PMDD, or pelvic floor dysfunction, don't receive the stream of funding for research and new treatments that other conditions do, despite affecting up to half the population."

- Just 100 years ago, care was based on the misguided theory that menstruation was a pathology.

- The one piece of the story that we seldom hear is that "women of reproductive age are in the minority in this country and are more vulnerable than just about any age group," according to Margaret Atwood. We must help this group write their stories.

- Michael Murphy wrote about the forced sterilization of young women of color, which continues to be practiced in some immigration centers.

Sisterly Guidance

Start a red-tent circle or another women's group where you can gather with friends to share information that might help you experience this life event in a more positive way. Set up ceremonies to honor the transitional stages and invite your daughters and mothers to attend. If you are a woman of color, consider your work to be history (or herstory).

Motherhood: Being Mothered, Mothering, or Caretaking

The story of the fragile relationship between mother and daughter comes to light in the estrangement of Rebecca Walker and her mother, feminist author Alice Walker, which lasted for several years and kept Alice from being present during the birth of her first grandchild. Rebecca blamed the break in their relationship on their differences over motherhood, saying, "My mum taught me that children enslave women...that children are millstones around your neck, and the idea that motherhood can make you blissfully happy is a complete fairy tale."

Walker's much-publicized anti-Semitic remarks following the divorce of Rebecca's father, a Jewish attorney, may have added to the breakdown in their relationship. Theirs is not an uncommon tale of the complexities that have caused the relationship between mothers and daughters to become an endangered one.

Many of us have struggled to navigate a relationship with our mothers, only to discover a similar tension developing with our own daughters, as they begin to individuate and claim their own identities. While much has been written about this battle by experts on family and children, we need more stories in the words of women, who are brave enough to pose questions about the social and cultural conditions that contribute to this fragile relationship and consider how the idealized notion of motherhood may be part of the problem.

This section asks you to write about motherhood from two perspectives:

1) As a mother
2) As a daughter

As you write, you may see both yourself and your mother differently. Allow that to happen and write about your revelations as they come to you.

Sisterly Guidance

Do not share this with anyone except members of your writing group. Be sure you feel safe with this group because they may have different interpretations of motherhood. If writing about your relationship with your mother, I advise not to share your story with her. This is your private declaration, and you do not need to feel like you're being surveilled as you write. Be prepared to have a wide range of feelings, including grief. Many of us lost mothers before we were able to resolve the tensions between us and this can be quite painful. Be gentle with yourself. You may wish to write this story in the form of a letter to your mother. Keep what you write and return to it in the future.

Writing Prompts on Being a Mother

1. Write a story about your feelings of mothering. If you are a mother, discuss an experience that made you feel a certain way. If you have trouble finding the words, read some of the sources included in this section.

2. Write about a time when you felt you were being judged for failing to live up to the norms imposed on mothers. For example, do you feel pressured to follow so-called "momfluencers" on social media and, if so, how does this affect your feelings about your mothering practices?

3. Write your own motherhood manifesto, listing the things you need and want.

Writing Prompts on Writing About Your Mother-Daughter Relationship

1. Write a story about your relationship with your mother.

2. Write a story about your mother's relationship with her mother.

Additional Thoughts

- Being a mother is regarded in this culture as the most desirable role for all women and books on motherhood focus almost entirely on the health and happiness mothers can provide to their children, but little has been written about the experience for the mother. Dr. Gertrude Lyons, author of *Rewrite the Mother Code: From Sacrifice to Stardust - A Cosmic Approach to Motherhood,* challenges this model saying, it is "broken, limited, constricting, and disempowering." We're expected to cope with "frantic hormonal fluctuations, the lack of sleep, the constant giving of yourself whilst getting nothing back." And we are socialized to believe we love this role and shamed for any doubts we express.

- Living in a capitalist economy has made family struggles vulnerable to being commercialized, resulting in a growing field of marriage and family therapists who have a vested interest in defining interactions as binaries, such as victim/perpetrator. Unfortunately, mother-daughter relationships have been influenced by this attitude and some believe it's encouraged the growth of estrangement ideology, or the tendency to cut off relationships between family members.

- Clarissa Pinkola Estes writes in her book, *Women Who Run with The Wolves,* about the ancient practice in which tribes of women gathered in circles to allow older mothers to nurture younger ones through a woman-to-woman conversation. Mature age women, usually grandmothers, aunts, and other women in the community, shared their knowledge and wisdom with new mothers, spreading out the responsibility for mothering. As a communal form of mothering, this eased the burden and loneliness of the mother but, when the nuclear family became the norm, this ritual was lost.

- Most of us were mothered by women who were oppressed, silenced, and socialized to believe in motherhood as the most sacred experience possible. Women who were expected to fulfill an impossible role alone, a role once shared by an entire tribe of women and to do so without being paid for our labor. As daughters, we may have felt the resentment our mothers carried for these sexist expectations; yet we were encouraged to take part in their oppression by refusing to see our mothers as human beings.

- For an interesting blog post on the power of social media to affect the feelings of mothers, please check out "The Social Media Mom" in the Works Cited section.

Adoption

In the Old Testament story of Moses, we are told about the young mother, a Hebrew woman living in slavery, who leaves her infant son Moses in a basket in the Nile River. The story unfolds with his discovery by the Pharaoh's daughter who takes him home and raises him in a wealthy, powerful family. Most of us read the story for its characterization of a powerful God who asks Moses to return to his people and lead them to the promised land. As a Biblical story, it highlights a dominant narrative about the divine selection of a prophet, while it downplays the complexities faced by the child, the adoptive family, and the birth family. Complexities such as the trauma caused by separation of the child and birth mother, and the demands placed on the adoptive family are not included in the story. Less commonly understood issues, such as identity, race, and social class, are also left out of the narrative. This section asks you to write about your adoption journey using prompts that should help you consider these often-over-looked issues. The prompts ask you to re-see the experience by looking at the unique ways each member of the triad experiences adoption.

The Experience of the Adopted Child

America leads the world in the adoption of children. Considered to be a desirable way to bring children and parents together, adoption is one of the most rewarding experiences for everyone involved. As the understanding of human psychology evolves, the difficulties experienced by members of the adoption triad are becoming more clear. Advancements in technology, as well as a shift in social attitudes, have led to a more holistic approach that considers the needs of the adoptive child, adoptive parents, and the birth mother.

For example, more attention is now given to the trauma that comes from the initial attachment disruption caused by the separation of the mother and infant. Dr. Gabor Mate, who speaks from his own experience, explains the trauma felt by the infant caused by the sudden break. He said, "For nine months, they heard the voice of the mother, registered the heartbeat, attuning with the biorhythms with the mother. The expectation is that it will continue. This is utterly broken for the adopted child. We don't have sufficient appreciation for what happens to that infant and how to compensate for it."

Sisterly Guidance

Be so loving to yourself as you write about your life as an adoptee. Do not pressure yourself by sharing your work with anyone and try not to silence yourself as you write. Searchangels.org is a national non-profit organization where you can find help in locating a birth mother/father and in joining a community of others who share your experience.

Writing Prompts for Adoptees

1. Write your story. Tell what you remember, what you feel, what you suspect may be true. Allow yourself to speculate or guess. You may want to find help from an ancestral researcher to gather background information. Retell the story in a poem or create a collage that captures your experience.

2. Write a letter to your birth mother and father. Ask them what you'd like to know about your life, your biological family, your heritage. Ask about their decision to relinquish you.

The Experience of the Adoptive Mother

Moses' adoptive mother's story is told in the context of her role in raising a child who became a prophet, lifting the Hebrew slaves out of bondage and bringing forth the Ten Commandments. Yet, although she saved a child from danger and cared for him from infancy to adulthood, her own journey is never shared. Her silence deprives us of an account of an adoptive mother's experience during a time of political and cultural upheaval, a story that might have provided valuable insight for adoptive mothers in our contemporary world. It also highlights one of the defining features of adoption: the broken story. In the words of one adoptive mother, "The whole reason adoption exists as a societal construct is as a direct response to a specific traumatic experience that has disrupted the plot of the 'main story.'" If Moses' adoptive mother could be here to share her story, I wonder what she'd tell us. Can you see yourself in her story?

Sisterly Guidance

This is not an easy subject and I strongly encourage you to write while working with a group (preferably, a group of other adoptive mothers). The experience of motherhood is very complex and adding adoption to the mix adds layers of stories that you may not be able to see as you write. Indeed, you may be carrying stories you have no way of knowing, so be very kind to yourself. You have done a selfless wonderful thing by raising this child. I strongly recommend that you honor yourself by treating your story as a piece of precious history. You might consider printing it on delicate paper and keeping it in a box tied with a beautiful bow.

Writing Prompts for an Adoptive Mother

1. Write the story of your journey as an adoptive mother. Include as much detail as you can remember. Explain why you chose to adopt a child. How do you feel about your decision now? Re-tell your story in a poem or make a collage. Be sure to acknowledge your courage and your devotion to the relationship.

2. Write a letter to your adopted child.

3.

Write a letter to your child's birth mother.

The Experience of the Birth Mother

Moses' birth mother, Jochebed, made the heart-rending decision to give up her child to save his life when the King ordered the death of all Hebrew boys. Her story is not told in the Bible–not in her words. Portrayed as a faithful follower of God, Jochebed's story is subsumed under the divine narrative told in Exodus. Until recently, very little attention has been paid to the experiences of women who relinquish their infants for adoption. Their experiences of grief, ambiguous loss, and identity struggles have been buried under stories of shame and judgment. This was more common before the availability of modern birth control methods, but the stigma still exists.

This section asks you to reflect on your decision to give up a child by stepping into a judgment-free zone where you can use your imagination to create a beautiful written piece that honors you as a creator, a birth mother. As you write, allow yourself to explore the depth of your feelings about your loss, as well as your desires for your child's future. In this zone, allow yourself to be free of outside influences and voices that may have judged you. Write about yourself as a heroine. Treat your decision as carefully as Jochebed might have done when she left her child in the basket she wove to carry him down the river. The space you create to write your story is large enough to hold all that you feel.

Sisterly Guidance

As you write in response to the prompts, allow yourself to be as expressive as possible. You may want to write from a second person point-of-view or to write a poem about the experience. You may also begin with a collage. Be aware that this is some of the heaviest work you'll ever do, so be gentle with yourself. You are very courageous to write about this experience and your story will add to the collection of untold tales by birth mothers.

Writing Prompts for a Birth Mother

1. Write about your decision to relinquish your child. Did you feel prepared to do so and were you pressured or shamed into doing so?

2. Write a story about your child, whether you have contact or not. If you do not have contact with your child, write about your journey to find the child. Or write about your decision not to locate him/her/them.

Additional Thoughts

- In recent years, much has been written about the birth trauma experienced by infants and adopted children. They now have many more sources for support as they work through experiences, such as fear of abandonment and trust. Still, some struggle with articulating their experiences, either because the most traumatic occurred before they had language or because they have been silenced by adoptive families, who have discouraged them from seeking their biological family members.

- A 1999 study by Origins Canada found that 89% of birth mothers considered relinquishing a child to be an "extremely" traumatic experience. Ninety-four percent said they did not have adequate counseling at the time of relinquishment, and 85% reported being misled about the lasting psychological effects they could expect to encounter.

Mental Health

In Charlotte Perkins Gilman's story, "The Yellow Wallpaper," a mother writes as a way to come to terms with the despair that's hit her, as she struggles with postpartum depression and being confined to a small room. She writes in search of the words to express her feelings. She writes to understand her condition. She writes until her husband forbids her from doing so. With no one to interact with, no outside stimulus, or books to read, she becomes preoccupied with the yellow papered walls, believing that a woman has been trapped beneath the wallpaper who wants to be freed. Charlotte Perkins Gilman's story is considered a classic example of a woman's struggle to restore her voice, as she fights against the forces that demoralize her and the stigma against depression that adds to her suffering. When this story was written, depression was not understood as it is today and, at that time, it was not unusual for a woman to be labeled as hysterical, to be pathologized and deemed hard to control. She might be diagnosed with "moral insanity" for just about any kind of behavior that made men uncomfortable. Attitudes have changed over the years, but this history weighs on women who still feel the shadow of these biases.

In this section, you are invited to see yourself as both an individual who may be struggling with an emotional concern–perhaps, even working with a therapist–and as a member of a larger community of women coping with social, political, and global threats to our mental health.

I want to emphasize that this section is not intended to be therapy, nor to replace the relationship you may have with your own therapist. The prompts ask you to respond to the way you use your voice to navigate your relationship with your counselor, pastor, or therapist, as well as to explore the psychological impact of social and cultural conditions and attitudes on how you see yourself as a consumer of mental health.

Sisterly Guidance

This is a section where you can use writing to explore and try out ideas and responses. Do not be afraid to go against mainstream ideas about mental health and therapy if they do not fit your experience. Be very gentle with yourself. If the entire story is too frightening or you begin to have symptoms of dissociation, stop and seek support. When you return to the story, tell it in pieces, using a timer to control the amount of time you spend writing. Ground yourself in the present. Also, consider using the prompts about world conditions to foster a discussion with your family. This could be a very healthy way to help your children begin to process the trauma they are witnessing in the world.

Writing Prompts About Mental Health

1. Write about your current relationship with your therapist, spiritual director, or counselor.

2. Write a story about yourself as someone who is witnessing global violence and trying to make sense of it without becoming overwhelmed. Or, write about how your experience as a witness to the suffering in the world is affecting your life.

3. If you are a woman of color, write about the way discrimination and racist attitudes have influenced your sense of well-being in the world. Protect yourself by being careful whom you share your work with.

4. Write about a time you felt a therapist said something to you that didn't align with your perception. Did you express this to the therapist? Was the therapist accepting? Or, write about a time when you disagreed with a therapist or set boundaries in your session. How did you express your expectations? How did you feel about doing so?

5. If you've been assigned any type of label, write about the impact it's had on you. For example, do you feel this label has become a form of your identity? Do you introduce yourself using this label?

6. Write about your goal in maintaining good mental health. Have you considered your goal to be one of liberation, rather than one of healing or fixing?

7. Write about a time when you discussed the impact of being silenced with your therapist.

8. Write about an experience with a mental health support group. If you felt silenced or unheard/unseen by the group, write about it.

9. Write about the effect of living under the Trump administration on your sense of well-being and mental health. Keep in mind that you are recording your experience, and you are contributing to history with your story.

Additional Thoughts

- Adding to individual struggles, we are facing a "collective trauma," caused by exploitation and othering—including systemic racism, misogyny, and anthropocentrism. The Climate Psychology Alliance of North America has identified these as contributing factors to a decline in well-being and provides resources for "meeting isolation, societal alienation, and helplessness with solidarity, connection, compassion, and care."

- Dr. Jennifer Mullan, author of *Decolonizing Therapy: Oppression, Historical Trauma & Politicizing Your Practice,* writes that fear, anger, and helplessness are normal feelings under current world conditions, which "are not isolated tragedies. They reflect systems designed to oppress, displace, and silence."

- Therapist Patricia Duggan writes about the effects on the body and mind for women living under "fascism." In her words, the "body under fascism learns to shrink, suppress, obey. It's taught that control equals safety and that feeling is dangerous. But the body remembers. It remembers movement, care, resistance....Fascism may live in systems, but liberation lives in the body."

Ancestral Stories

When I wrote my memoir, *Story Carrier: A Collection of Tales of the Disappeared*, my goal was to free myself of the anger I carried about my relationship with my mother. However, in researching family history on the maternal side of my family, I discovered a story that connected me to a great-grandmother who died more than a hundred years ago. In discovering her tale, I knew my work would not be as simple as I expected. When my great-grandmother was a young mother, she picked up a gun and shot her father. She lost custody of her child (my grandmother) and, although never charged with a crime, she was locked up in a mental institution for the rest of her life. My grandmother was told that her mother had abandoned her, which wounded her deeply. She died without knowing the full story. In fact, no one in my family knew this story. No one knows the reason behind my great-grandmother's actions; yet her story has influenced the lives of all the women in my family, including my mother, her sisters, and me.

The prompts in this section are intended to help you begin to write about ancestors whose life stories have impacted your own–even if you do not know their stories. Like me, you may encounter a tale so powerful, it may have influenced family dynamics in ways you could not have imagined before learning the story. Like me, you may see your life mirrored in the lives of ancestors whom you've never met.

Sisterly Guidance

These stories carry across generations for years and their impact can be felt before you have the words to articulate them. Or, you may simply not know the story that explains the feelings you have about your family. Prepare to be both surprised and, in some instances, upset by what you discover. Go slowly. Talk with family members. Be prepared for some family members to have negative reactions to your writing and exploration. Be assured that you are doing the right thing; you are liberating other ancestors who have been silenced. Again, be very gentle with yourself. If the entire story is too frightening or you begin to have symptoms of dissociation, stop and seek support. When you return to the story, tell it in pieces, using a timer to control the amount of time you spend writing. Ground yourself in the present.

Writing Prompts for Ancestral Stories

1. Write a story about an ancestor about whom you've been told to remain silent.

2. Write a story about an ancestor your family refuses to acknowledge.

3. Interview your mother, grandmother, and/or other women in your family and write their stories. Invite them to join you in the writing process.

Additional Thoughts

- Psychotherapist Dr. Galit Atlas, whose work involves following the clues uncovering untold family stories, says we all live in the shadow of our ancestors' life experiences. Yet, as a society focused primarily on the nuclear family, neither do we know their stories nor do we understand their power to shape our lives. In a world that diminishes us by silencing our stories, we need to establish a connection to the ancestors whose stories we carry in our bones.

- Educator Desiree Stephens writes that re-connecting to our ancestral tribe helps us survive social isolation and defy oppression, and she suggests telling ancestral stories as a defense against efforts to silence us.

Workplace Experiences of Harassment and Discrimination

Note: This section is near the end of the book for a reason. I suspect that many of you are carrying stories about being silenced in the workplace or have experienced it in various forms, such as discrimination, microaggressions, harassment, or having to cope with an oppressive or toxic work culture. Your story will help change this narrative for all women.

Harassment

Kelly Stonelake recently filed a sexual harassment lawsuit against Meta, which owns Facebook and Instagram, after 15 years of experiencing harassment and near-assault on the job. Stonelake was fired in 2023, as head of the company's Horizon program, after raising concerns about racism in a video game created by Meta. As soon as she spoke up, she was exposed to unbearable behavior by her male colleagues, including having her "crotch grabbed, screamed at, [and] told to have sex with [her] boss for a promotion." She argues that filing the suit is more than a legal action against sexual harassment; it's a charge against "toxic and discriminatory environments [that] aren't just wrong, they're anti-innovation. Hating women hurts everyone." While her lawsuit may not result in compensating Stonelake for her suffering, she has taken the first step in restoring her autonomy by speaking up in a legal forum and assuming narrative control over the story.

Women of color hit an impenetrable barrier in professional work settings, where they hold only 4% of management positions, compared to 19% held by white women and 68% by white men. They face barriers to career advancement based on gender and race, imposed by organizational cultures, policies, and practices.

This section asks you to consider your own experiences on the job, including any form of discrimination, acts of harassment, or even microaggressions. These are common experiences shared by most women who are employed, even those who own their own businesses and work for themselves.

Sisterly Guidance

Writing about the workplace may be a bit intimidating for you; however, keep in mind that you do not have to take any action based on what you've written unless and until you decide to do so. These prompts should help you reflect on your work setting in a way that allows you the freedom to explore and deeply consider how you feel about it. You do not have to share your responses with anyone. If you ever decide that your work conditions are intolerable, you will have a record of your experience.

Writing Prompts About Workplace Experiences of Harassment and Discrimination

1. Write about an experience you've had involving harassment on the job.

2.

Share a story about the environment of your workplace. Include your experience of the presence of racist, sexist, or ageist attitudes.

3. If you work for yourself or own your own business, write about experiences you've had that made you feel diminished, silenced, or treated with disrespect.

4. Write about an experience you've had involving discrimination on your job.

5. Write about an experience you've had where you felt silenced on your job.

Additional Thoughts

- In a 2017 Pew Research Survey, 22 percent of women reported sexual harassment on the job. Speaking up about it may feel liberating, however it also brings the threat of losing one's job.
- Although Title VII of the Civil Rights Act made it illegal to discriminate against workers because of race, color, religion, sex, and national origin, the Pew Research Center reports that 42 percent of them have reported experiencing gender-based discrimination. Twenty-five percent reported earning less than a male coworker performing the same job. The likelihood of being discriminated against is greater when factors such as gender identity, sexuality, race, and ethnicity are considered.

Home (as a Worksite)

Henrik Ibsen's 1879 Norwegian play, "A Doll's House," tracks the privileged life of traditional wife Nora Helmer as she dances through her days, living a life that might seem ideal from the outside looking in. As the spouse of a bank manager, Nora performs her role as a beautiful wife and mother of gorgeous, clean-faced children, and she tends an absurdly over-decorated home. She also struggles to keep her husband from discovering a secret debt she owes to one of his employees. When the employee threatens to blackmail Nora by telling her husband about their financial arrangement, she begins to re-evaluate her marriage. Nora thinks about the lifestyle she has and its cost to her independence, such as the expectation that she play a diminished, silent role in the marriage and allow herself to be seen as a side character to her domineering, overbearing husband. Giving up her liberty has not been easy for her, but being threatened with humiliation and shame pushes her to the brink. Nora becomes so disillusioned that she chooses to walk out of the marriage, leaving behind her husband and children. In the final lines of the play, Nora literally slams the door on her role, rejecting societal norms that have demanded her silence, and she asserts control over her voice and agency.

Let's be honest. Home is a worksite for women, our place of employment where we are expected to be present every day, regardless of health or any other demands on our time. Home is a second job for most women and our labor is unpaid. Feminist Silvia Federici writes that domestic labor has been mostly ignored in this country, where the work of maintaining a home and caring for children still falls disproportionately to women.

This section is not intended to ask you to pick a side in the debate over women's labor, nor does it ask you to think about the way women have been socialized to desire living the life of traditional wives and mothers. But it does ask you to explore your feelings about your home as a worksite, where you give your time and energy, often at the expense of your own needs and your independence. The prompts ask you to see your home as both your sanctuary and your worksite.

Sisterly Guidance

Be as honest and clear as possible as you write. Allow yourself to rant, to scream, and to feel everything that comes up as you do so. Slam the door! Roar!

Writing Prompts for Writing About Home as a Worksite

1. Write about your work life, including your job as a homemaker.

2. Write about the arrangement in your home over the division of labor.

3. Write about the division of emotional labor involving maintaining your marriage (or relationship), as well as your relationship with children and other family members you provide for.

Additional Thoughts

- Oxfam recently reported that if women worldwide made minimum wage for the work they do around the house and caring for relatives, this work would have been valued at nearly $11 trillion.
- Public policy scholar Marilyn Waring describes the current arrangement, in which the economy exploits the labor of women, as a way of disappearing those who perform activities, such as caring for elderly relatives or newborns, shopping, and cooking. The patriarchy benefits from dismissing the difficult work conducted by women. When our unpaid labor is seen through this lens, it's clear that women are not only unheard and unseen, we may also be colonized by an economy that depends on our unpaid labor.

Religious/Spiritual Spaces

Sue Monk Kidd writes in her memoir, *Dance of the Dissident Daughter: A Woman's Journey from Christian Tradition to the Sacred Feminine,* "There is no place so awake and alive as the edge of becoming. But more than that, birthing the kind of woman who can authentically say, 'My soul is my own,' and then embody it in her life, her spirituality, and her community is worth the risk and hardship." In her novel *The Secret Life of Bees,* Kidd tells the story of the spiritual coming of age of Lily, who, after losing her own mother, develops a relationship with three sisters–women of color–who introduce her to the divine feminine. The story tells how the loss of the feminine voice in the Bible has diminished the fullness of women's spiritual experience.

As you write in this section, consider your own religious experience. Has it been shaped by the presence of a dominant male voice? Or by a religious history that includes mainly stories of men? You may have felt unseen or excluded in your faith community. Or you may have found a way to include the voice of the divine feminine in your own personal spiritual practice. You are the expert of your own experience and your story, and your voice is important to the evolving awareness of the story of spirituality.

Sisterly Guidance

Writing about spiritual abuse is very tricky and requires that you surround yourself with supportive people who do not include your pastor or anyone in church leadership. If possible, speak with someone who can serve as an advocate for your interests and help you navigate powerful emotions. As a spiritual director, I have discovered that church can be a wonderful source of comfort, but it can also be one of the most hurtful experiences a woman can have. Be aware that writing about this may cause you to feel overwhelmed and frightened, and I encourage you to trust your intuition. If you feel something has been harmful to you, you are probably right. Pace yourself when writing about these experiences. If the entire story is too uncomfortable, stop and seek support. When you return to the story, tell it in pieces, using a timer to control the amount of time you spend writing. Ground yourself in the present and practice somatic exercises to help you feel safe.

Writing Prompts for Exploring Voice in Religious/Spiritual Spaces

1. Write about an experience you've had in your place of worship or with a church/spiritual leader where you felt ignored, unrecognized, or uncomfortable. Explain your discomfort.

2. Write about any experience you've had when you felt excluded by any form of worship. This can include liturgical practices, the heavy use of stories of men's spiritual experiences, or the lack of women's voices in services.

3.

Share your feelings about whether or not you feel your life is reflected in the tales told about women in the Bible, the Torah, Quran, or any other collection of religious/spiritual stories.

4. Write about a time when you've felt spiritually abused. (For example, told you were sinful, told to repent, or asked to obey a male church leader's requests.)

5. Write about any spiritual experience that felt coercive. This may include feeling judged or told you have committed a sin or violated a religious "rule." It may involve being told you have not obeyed scripture, or have failed to acknowledge the presence of God or a higher being in the way expected by your church. It may include being told how to behave in your marriage or in other areas of your life. Be courageous as you work through this prompt. Spiritual abuse occurs in very subtle ways.

6. Write about a time when you have felt confused about your faith. This may have been because you were told to believe "God has a plan," when you were struggling with events in your life. Or, it may have been more subtle, such as being told that your suffering is a challenge to your faith.

Additional Thoughts

- When wounded by an experience in the faith community, you may experience the following, according to HappyWholeWay.com:

    1. A negative sense of self
    2. An inability to access your own inner authority
    3. Trouble thinking for yourself
    4. Lack of connection to your sense of autonomy
    5. Grief and loneliness after losing community
    6. Trouble navigating your emotions

- Male dominance in places of worship across all faiths cannot be denied. Soraya Chemaly writes, "Given that 100% of official Catholic priests, 99% of Islamic clerics, 100% of Orthodox rabbis, and 90% of Buddhist leadership roles are filled by men, it seems relevant, a laughable understatement, to center religion and its ripple effects fairly regularly. Male supremacy in religion sanctifies the intimate, political, economic, and social systems that maintain inequalities. Religion affects everyone, regardless of personal beliefs or participation."

- Rev Karla Kamstra is an interfaith/interspiritual minister who works with those trying to identify and come to terms with religious trauma, as well as those in search of a spiritual community that more closely meets their needs. Her book, *Deconstructing: Leaving Church, Finding Faith* is a recommended guide for anyone in the process of change.

- **Resource: Visit HappyWholeWay.com, a website that offers a program for recovery from religious harm.**

Grief

The book *Sadako and the Thousand Paper Cranes* by Eleanor Coerr tells of the true story of the young Japanese girl who survived the bombing of Hiroshima, Japan, only to develop leukemia several years later as a likely result of radiation poisoning. While hospitalized, the Red Cross Youth Club gave Sadako an origami crane. Her father explained the symbolism, telling her, "Japanese folklore says that a crane can live for a thousand years, and a person who folds an origami crane for each year of a crane's life will have their wish granted." Inspired by the myth, Sadako collected thousands of pieces of paper and began to fold cranes, hoping to be granted her wish for restored health. Sadly, she passed away at the age of 12, surrounded by more than 1,300 origami cranes she and her friends folded. Her childhood friends raised money for a statue of Sadako that now stands in the Hiroshima Peace Memorial Park, with a plaque that reads: "This is our cry. This is our prayer. Peace in the world." Her story is a tribute to the power of art to inspire stories that reach beyond our own lives to touch others. It is a story that allows one to imagine a link to eternity.

In this country, we do not allow the time or space to fully grieve loss. As Americans, we are encouraged to move on, to return to a life of productivity as soon as possible. Although we have an industry that helps us when we've lost a loved one, their work is aimed at release or letting go quickly, in ritualized ways. But grieving is about loving and about remembering, and writing offers a method for doing both. In *Remembering Well*, Sarah York writes, "As they participate, they remember. As they remember, they grieve. As they grieve, they love."

The prompts in this section are focused on helping you write stories in honor of your losses, as well as to give voice to your loved one by telling your story about them. It encourages you to remember them by seeing them in your stories.

Sisterly Guidance

Be very gentle with yourself. If the entire story is too unsettling, stop and seek support. Also, consider that deep feelings, including anger or betrayal, may not be pathological. They may be a sign that your story wants to take you deeper. Thank the story for trusting you to be its carrier.

Writing Prompts for Writing About Grief

1. Write the story of the one you've lost. Include a photograph. Make a collage. Sketch a picture. Consider creating a website to honor and celebrate your loved one.

2. Write a letter to your lost loved one. You may want to ask your loved one to speak to you, in a dream, a vision, or through a new story. Open yourself up to possibilities that you cannot imagine.

Section 4:
Recognition–Honoring Your Hard Work

Writing a (Wo)manifesto for Unsilencing the Self

Recommendations for Further Reading

Writing a (Wo)manifesto For Unsilencing the Self

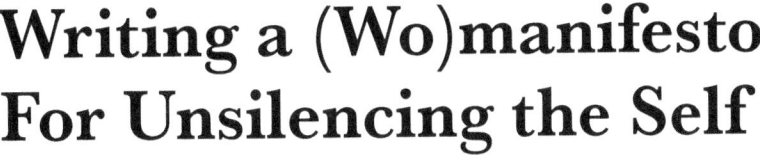

Congratulations! You've made it to the part of the journey where you can reward yourself. Whether you completed every section of the workbook or you've jumped ahead for the fun part, acknowledge the courage and stamina it took for you to arrive here. This section invites you to look back on all you've written, and to see the new understandings you've reached about yourself. It asks you to begin to think about how you'd like to change the way you're treated in the world by stating your expectations that you be seen and heard.

The (Wo)manifesto I've created for you is meant to help you declare your needs as a woman who is in charge of your story. A woman who is writing to restore your autonomy and reclaim your sovereignty. I suggest reading it over before you begin to work. Then, sit with all that you've written in the previous sections and allow yourself to imagine what you'd like to change. Allow yourself to name your needs and to give words to your desires you now see in yourself. Use the (Wo)manifesto to step into the new world you are making by writing to express the changes you'd like to see in your life. This can include changes in your own behavior, or expectations you may have for family members, friends, co-workers, supervisors, church leaders, therapists, doctors, and any other professionals you have contact with.

Keep in mind that as you write, you are creating a document for all women. You are drawing a roadmap for other women to follow on their way out of the wilderness of silence. Silencing may have felt like an individual experience, but we all have a profound stake in writing stories that can connect us to one another. When you've written as much as you want to write, stop and celebrate!

I, _____, feel _____

_____

_____

_____

_____

_____

_____

_____

_____

_____

_____

_____

_____

about my experiences of being silenced, dismissed, erased, or made invisible in my life.

When my family fails to hear me, I feel……

_____
_____
_____
_____
_____
_____
_____
_____

When I'm not seen or heard in the workplace, I feel……

_____
_____
_____
_____
_____
_____
_____
_____

The one big story I want to share while I'm still in this lifetime is……

_____
_____
_____
_____
_____
_____
_____
_____

The story I've had the most difficult time sharing is……

_____

_____

_____

_____

_____

_____

_____

_____

_____

The story that made me feel most uncomfortable listening to is……

_____

_____

_____

_____

_____

_____

_____

_____

_____

_____

I want my spouse/partner to hear me when I talk about……

_____

_____

_____

_____

_____

_____

_____

_____

_____

I want my children to listen to me when I talk about......

_____
_____
_____
_____
_____
_____
_____
_____
_____

I want my boss and co-workers to know......

_____
_____
_____
_____
_____
_____
_____
_____
_____
_____

I wish someone would understand me when I talk about......

_____
_____
_____
_____
_____
_____
_____
_____
_____
_____

I feel closer to my friends when I can share my story about......

_____

_____

_____

_____

_____

_____

_____

_____

_____

One story I want my family and friends to know is......

_____

_____

_____

_____

_____

_____

_____

_____

_____

_____

I will begin to listen to my body by......

_____

_____

_____

_____

_____

_____

_____

_____

_____

I will begin to notice and be attentive to my intuition daily by......

_____

_____

_____

_____

_____

_____

_____

_____

I will use discernment when it comes to labor in the home beginning with......

_____

_____

_____

_____

_____

_____

_____

_____

I will take care of my sense of well-being in the world (or mental health) by......

_____

_____

_____

_____

_____

_____

_____

_____

I will try to become aware of efforts to shame me when......

_____

_____

_____

_____

_____

_____

_____

_____

I will ask my doctor to......

_____

_____

_____

_____

_____

_____

_____

_____

_____

I will honor my soul by......

_____

_____

_____

_____

_____

_____

_____

_____

I will feed my need for art, music, creativity by……

_____
_____
_____
_____
_____
_____
_____
_____

I will ask a person close to me to listen to this story below, which I've never before shared.

_____
_____
_____
_____
_____
_____
_____
_____

I'll listen deeply to myself, trying to hear the stories I'm carrying beginning with……

_____
_____
_____
_____
_____
_____
_____
_____

Recommendations for Further Reading

Apple, Rima. *Perfect Motherhood: Science and Childrearing.* Rutgers University Press, 2006.

Atlas, Galit. *Emotional Inheritance: A Therapist, Her Patients, and the Legacy of Trauma.* Little Brown & Company, 2022.

Bassist, Elissa. "Medical Gaslighting." *Hysterical,* 19 Jan. 2024, hystericalbook.substack. com/p/medical-gaslighting.

BBC News. "Margaret Atwood on gender, women's rights, and Roald Dahl revisions." *YouTube,* 17 Mar. 2023, youtube.com/watch?v=ZizYgXqwWcA.

Boggs, Grace Lee, and Scott Kurashige. *The Next American Revolution: Sustainable Activism for the Twenty-First Century.* University of California Press, 2012.

Bourke, Joanna. *Disgrace: Global Reflections on Sexual Violence.* Reaktion Books, 2022.

Brown, Lyn Mikel, and Carol Gilligan. *Meeting at the Crossroads: Women's Psychology and Girls' Development.* Harvard University Press, 1992.

Chemaly, Soraya. "It's 2025. Is This a Good Time to Talk About Male Supremacy and Feminist Refusals?" *Unmanned,* 28 Jan. 2025, sorayachemaly.substack.com/p/ its-2025-time-to-talk-about-male.

Chemaly, Soraya. *Rage Becomes Her: The Power of Women's Anger.* Atria Books, 2018.

Chideya, Farai. "Rebecca Walker Explains Rift with Mother, Alice." *News & Notes,* NPR, 9 July 2008, www.npr.org/2008/07/09/92373475/rebecca-walker-explains-rift-with-mother-alice.

Clark, Jane. *Story Carrier: A Collection of Tales of the Disappeared.* Writing Brave Press, 2024.

Climate Psychology Alliance North America. "Climate Psychology Alliance North America/ Organization for Climate-Aware Therapists." 2025, www.climatepsychology.us/.

Coerr, Eleanor. *Sadako and the Thousand Paper Cranes.* G. P. Putnam's Sons, 1977.

Coffey, Clare, et al. "Time to care: Unpaid and underpaid care work and the global inequality crisis." *Oxfam International*, Jan. 2020, oxfamilibrary.openrepository.com/bitstream/handle/10546/620928/bp-time-to-care-inequality-200120-summ-en.pdf.

Crawford, Martha. "A Glimpse." *What a Shrink Thinks*, 31 Jan. 2025, www.whatashrinkthinks.com/essays/a-glimpse.

Cutchin, Carli. "No, That Persistent Pain Is Not in Your Head." *Dame Magazine*, 7 Mar. 2024, www.damemagazine.com/2024/03/07/no-that-persistent-pain-is-not-in-your-he.

Davis, Angela Y. *Women, Race, and Class*. Penguin, 2019.

Dean, Jodi. "Silvia Federici: The exploitation of women and the development of capitalism." *Liberation School*, 10 Nov. 2020, www.liberationschool.org/silvia-federici-women-and-capitalism/.

Diamant, Anita. *The Red Tent*. St. Martin's Press, 1997.

Duggan, Patricia. "Practicing Care Under Trump: A Therapist's Reflection on Surviving State Violence." *PatRadicalTherapist*, 9 Feb. 2025, patradicaltherapist.substack.com/p/practicing-care-under-trump-a-therapists.

English, Alexandra. "What Happened Inside the Gisele Pelicot Trial: Long But Not Long Enough." *Marie Claire*, 20 Dec. 2024, www.marieclaire.com.au/news/who-is-gisele-pelicot-the-horrific-french-rape-case-explained/.

Estes, Clarissa Pinkola. *Women Who Run with the Wolves: Myths and Stories of the Wild Woman Archetype*. Ballantine Books, 1996.

Feldscher, Karen. "When Beauty Causes Harm." *Harvard T.H. Chan School of Public Health*, 21 Dec. 2022, hsph.harvard.edu/news/when-beauty-causes-harm/.

Feminist Legal Clinic. "Making Women's Unpaid Work Count." 11 May 2018, feministlegal.org/making-womens-unpaid-work-count-feminist-economics-pioneer-marilyn-waring-on-care-and-the-unfinished-feminist-re-volution/.

Gilligan, Carol. *In a Different Voice: Psychological Theory and Women's Development*. Harvard University Press, 2016.

Gilman, Charlotte Perkins. *The Yellow Wallpaper*. Martino Fine Books, 1892.

Happy Whole Way. www.happywholeway.com/. Accessed 20 Mar. 2025.

Ibsen, Henrik. *A Doll's House*, 1879.

Ikeda, Kaori, and Hayley Teasdale. "How Our Memory Develops." *Australian*

Academy Of Science, 29 Sept. 2021, www.science.org.au/curious/people-medicine/
how-memory-develops.

Imy, Kate, et al. "Unframing the Binary: Introducing Bodies Beyond Binaries." *Bodies
beyond Binaries: In Colonial and Postcolonial Asia,* edited by Kate Imy et al., Leiden
University Press, 2024, pp. 9–38, www.jstor.org/stable/jj.20856827.3.

Institute for Research on Male Supremacism. "What is Male Supremacism?" 2023, www.
theirms.org/what-is-male-supremacism.

Jourdon, Alexandre, et al. "Modeling Idiopathic Autism in Forebrain Organoids Reveals an
Imbalance of Excitatory Cortical Neuron Subtypes during Early Neurogenesis." *Nature
Neuroscience,* vol. 26, 2023, pp. 1505–1515, www.nature.com/articles/s41593-023-
01399-0.

Kamstra, Karla. *Deconstructing: Leaving Church, Finding Faith.* St. Martin's Essentials, 2024.

Kidd, Sue M. *Dance of the Dissident Daughter: A Woman's Journey from Christian Tradition
to the Sacred Feminine.* Harper, 2016.

Kidd, Sue M. *The Secret Life of Bees.* Penguin, 2003.

Kraft, Robert. "Why You Can't Remember Your Early Childhood: Memory May
Require a Language and a Sense of Self." *Psychology Today,* 22 Dec. 2023, www.
psychologytoday.com/intl/blog/defining-memories/202309/why-cant-we-remember-
our-early-childhood.

Lyons, Gertrude. *Rewrite the Mother Code: From Sacrifice to Stardust - A Cosmic Approach
to Motherhood.* Rise Books, 2025.

Manne, Kate. *Down Girl: The Logic of Misogyny.* Penguin Books, 2019.

Moore, Kate. "Declared Insane for Speaking Up: The Dark American History of Silencing
Women Through Psychiatry." *Time,* 22 June 2022, time.com/6074783/psychiatry-
history-women-mental-health/.

Morrison, Toni. *The Bluest Eye.* Holt, Rinehart and Winston, 1970.

Mullan, Jennifer. *Decolonizing Therapy: Oppression, Historical Trauma, and Politicizing
Your Practice.* W.W. Norton & Co, 2023.

Murphy, Michael. "The Troubling Past of Forced Sterilization of Black Women and
Girls in Mississippi and the South." *Mississippi Free Press,* 4 June 2021, www.
mississippifreepress.org/the-troubling-past-of-forced-sterilization-of-black-women-and-
girls-in-mississippi-and-the-south/.

National Domestic Violence Hotline, www.thehotline.org/. Accessed 5 Oct. 2024.

National Sexual Violence Resource Center, www.nsvrc.org/. Accessed 20 Sept. 2024.

Ng, Isaac, et al. "Medical Gaslighting: A New Colloquialism." *The American Journal of Medicine,* vol. 137, no. 10, 20 Oct. 2024, pp. 920-922, www.amjmed.com/article/S0002-9343(24)00396-6/.

Nurture Therapy. "The Social Media Mom: Why Social Media Impacts The Way We Feel." 29 Jun. 2018, nurture-therapy.com/blog/2018/6/29/the-social-media-mom-why-social-media-impacts-the-way-we-feel.

The OLLIE Foundation. "The Trauma of Relinquishment - Adoption, Addiction and Beyond." *YouTube,* 14 May 2021, youtube.com/watch?v=3CW_GdFG1KY&t=561s.

Origins Canada. "Adoption Trauma: The Damage to Relinquishing Mothers." 2010, www.originscanada.org/adoption-trauma-2/trauma_to_surrendering_mothers/adoption-trauma-the-damage-to-relinquishing-mothers.

Ouellette, Jeannine. "We Create, Therefore We Endure." *Writing in the Dark*, 10 Feb. 2025, writinginthedark.substack.com/p/we-create-therefore-we-endure.

Ovid. *Metamorphoses.* Edited by R. J. Tarrant. Oxford University Press, 2004. Oxford Classical Texts.

Parker, Kim, and Cary Funk. "Gender Discrimination Comes in Many Forms for Today's Woman." *Pew Research Center*, 14 Dec. 2017, www.pewresearch.org/short-reads/2017/12/14/gender-discrimination-comes-in-many-forms-for-todays-working-women/. Accessed 28 Aug. 2024.

Petersen, Sarah, and Kate Manne. "This Essay Made Me An Even Angrier Angry Feminist.

Progressive Feminism or Patriarchy - Which Is Worse??? (I'm So Tired)." *In Pursuit of Clean Countertops,* 4 Mar. 2025, sarapetersen.substack.com/p/this-essay-made-me-an-even-angrier.

Pinkishe Foundation. "The History of Menstruation: From Ancient Myths to Modern Science." 9 June 2024, www.pinkishe.org/blog-post/the-history-of-menstruation-from-ancient-myths-to-modern-science.

Potter, Beatrix. *The Tale of Peter Rabbit.* Frederick Warne, 1902.

Powers, Ann. "Taylor Swift's 'Tortured Poets' Is Written in Blood." *NPR Music*, 19 Apr. 2024, www.npr.org/2024/04/19/1245630721/taylor-swift-tortured-poets-department-revie.

Rein, Valerie. *Patriarchy Stress Disorder: The Invisible Inner Barrier to Women's Happiness and Fulfillment*. Lioncrest, 2019.

SheKnows. "Navigating Medical Gaslighting." www.sheknows.com/special-series/navigating-medical-gaslighting/.

Stephens, Desiree. "Dear White Women: This is Where the Work Begins." *Liberation Education Newsletter,* 6 Nov. 2024, desireebstephens.substack.com/p/dear-white-women-this-is-where-the.

Stonelake, Kelly. "Stonelake V. Meta." *OVERTURNED*, 4 Feb. 2025, overturned.substack.com/p/stonelake-v-meta.

Tang, Karen. *It's Not Hysteria: Everything You Need to Know About Your Reproductive Health (But Were Never Told)*. Flatiron Books, 2024.

Tweed, Anna, Ed. *The Arabian Nights*. New York, The Baker & Taylor Company, 1910.

United Nations Women. "Violence Against Women." 2025, interactive.unwomen.org/multimedia/infographic/violenceagainstwomen/en/index.html.

United States Department of Justice. "Improving Law Enforcement Response to Sexual Assault and Domestic Violence by Identifying and Preventing Gender Bias." 31 May 2022, www.justice.gov/d9/pages/attachments/2022/05/31/gender_bias_guidance.final_.pdf.

U.S. Equal Employment Opportunity Commission. "Women in the American Workforce." 12 Apr. 2023, www.eeoc.gov/special-report/women-american-workforce. Accessed 5 Dec. 2024.

Watson-Creed, Gaynor. "Gaslighting in Academic Medicine: Where Anti-Black Racism Lives." *Canadian Medical Association Journal*, vol. 194, no. 42, 31 Oct. 2022, pp. 1451-1454, https://doi.org/10.1503/cmaj.212145.

Wobick-Segev, Sarah E. "Beyond Binaries: Economics of the Family." *American Jewish History*, vol. 103, no. 4, 2019, pp. 527–29. *JSTOR*, www.jstor.org/stable/26863508.

Women's Resource Center to End Domestic Violence. "Racial Justice and Domestic Violence." 2025, www.wrcdv.org/racial-justice.

World Health Organization. "Maternal Mortality." 26 Apr. 2024, www.who.int/news-room/fact-sheets/detail/maternal-mortality. Accessed 21 Mar. 2025.

York, Sarah. *Remembering Well: Rituals for Celebrating Life and Mourning Death*. Jossey-Bass, 2000.

Acknowledgements

Virginia Woolf said, "For most of history, anonymous was a woman." Her words echoed in my mind as I put together this writing workbook, pushing myself to confront my own experience with the forces that silenced me, reminding me just how much courage is required of all women to come out of anonymity. I am grateful for all the women—some famous and others who are not well known–who laid the foundation that allows me to do this work of accompanying women on the journey of becoming visible.

I'd like to publicly thank them. Brooke Adams Law, the owner of Writing Brave Press, inspired me to trust my voice by stepping in to channel the spirit of my book when I lost touch with its desire to be written. Brooke's gift for intuitive writing pushed me through long spells of writer's block, when I was unsure that I was headed in the right direction. Her team reinforced my belief that women can create a peaceful working environment while achieving a beautiful product. I have deeply appreciated Meghan Dippel and Meghan Muldowney, and Michelle Argyle Park for their help in putting the finishing touches on this project.

I'm indebted to members of my own writing group who challenged me on the basic concepts of silencing on which this workbook is grounded. I am especially grateful for Mary Aebischer, Sharon Wilson, Devany LeDrew, Debby Hackett, and Mary Margaret Draughton for their input. In particular, Mary Aebischer helped me articulate my own position on the intersectionality of oppression of women which disadvantages some women over others.

The summer before I finished this book, I took my eleven-year-old granddaughter, Melis, to see the Broadway musical, "Suffs,"the all-woman play about the battle waged by the Suffragettes to secure approval of the 19 amendment, giving some women the right to vote. I wanted her to know the names of the women who fought for passage, and I believed it would help her appreciate the importance of having a black/Asian woman run for president during her lifetime. As the story unfolded on the stage, I saw a different tale emerge about the way black women had been excluded by leaders of the movement. By women I had held up as heroines. When the actress playing journalist Ida B. Wells sang "Wait My Turn," I broke into tears.

My granddaughter saw my reaction and put her arm around me. We didn't discuss it on that day but, in hindsight, I know we shared a moment of clarity about the silencing of women that was overlooked in the original story. Together, we witnessed the exclusion and silencing of blacks from the vote, told in the stories of women whose names had been erased from the original account. I'm grateful to my granddaughter for recognizing the weight of the moment and responding with care.

When I returned to this book, I re-focused my goal, turning it into a call-to-arms to all women to step forward, refuse to be oppressed by being silenced, and to become aware of our failure to honor the stories told by all women. As bell hooks wrote in her seminal work, *Talking Back: Thinking Feminist, Thinking Black,* "moving from silence into speech is for the oppressed, the colonized, the exploited, and those who stand and struggle side by side a gesture of defiance that heals, that makes new life and new growth possible." I am deeply grateful for hooks' work.

I do have one man to acknowledge and that is my husband, Larry, who has stood by my side, supporting me through months of long nights as I wrote and revised. Without his love and encouragement, I might not have completed any of my work. I might have succumbed to the internal messages telling me I needed to be less political, or to use softer language. On a daily basis, he reminded me to use my voice while he walked alongside me in a patriarchal world that threatens to make me invisible.